WOMAN

BEING ON THE WRONG SIDE OF MINISTRY

A DIARY OF AN EX PASTOR'S WIFE

LINDA Y. FOSTER

Copyright @ 2020 by Linda Y. Foster
All scriptures unless otherwise listed are from the King James Bible

Quotes from: The Late Dr. Myles Munroe: Steps to Writing and Publishing your Book

Book Cover Picture and Cover Design
Hoskey Photography

Makeup by: Yvonne Hoskey

All rights reserved
Published in the United States by
Linda Y. Foster Publishing

DEDICATION

To my Parents: The late Mr. Douglas Edward Mickens Sr. and Mrs. Clara Lee Williams Mickens

Thank you for giving me life; without the two of you there would be no me.

Even though I was not raised by my father, I still thank God that he gave me life.

My mother whom I love dearly and appreciate to the moon and back, I thank you for all your wisdom and knowledge.

I have always admired you for your strength and your tenacity to keep going even when you could have given up. I thank you for your example of a hard-working single parent, it is because of you that I will never give up. Thank you for believing in me, even when I did not believe it for myself.

To my Grandparents: The late Mr. Odell Williams and The late Mrs. Lucille Glover Williams

I thank you both for your wisdom, stability, and work ethics that were taught to me from a young girl.
I can still hear you both speaking, especially during some of the hardest struggles. Today as I reflect your wise counsel spoken in my hearing, I also planted in my three sons.

I can only pray that they will meditate on them as I did, that in their difficult times your wise counsel will encourage them as well. I am forever grateful for my upbringing and lineage.

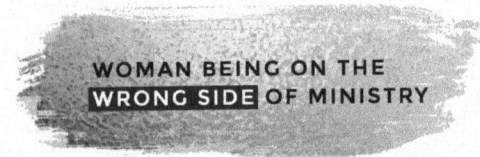

Foreword

I first met Linda Y. Foster and her family while stationed in Giessen, West Germany approximately thirty-three years ago. I witnessed her rise from newborn believer to Co-Pastor and Executive Pastor of a thriving church. She has always demonstrated the epitome of leadership and hospitality. One of the things that I have always appreciated about her was her ability to be honest and to stand up for right. I have always known Linda to stand firm in her teaching and ministering of the doctrine of the Lord Jesus Christ. As a Licensed Marriage and Family Therapist, I believe "Being on the Wrong Side of Ministry" is a must read for both men and women pursuing a path towards professional Christian ministry. In her book, Linda describes many pitfalls that hinder those called to serve, and if heeded, her book can assist the reader in avoiding mistakes that are routinely experienced in ministerial practice.

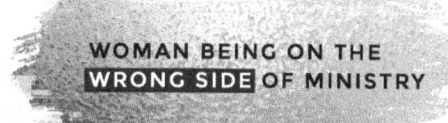

In her writing, she has taken the reader along with her on her path of challenges and recovery. She has provided thoughtful insight into her own and common mistakes made in the Body of Christ as we endeavor to pursue the Will of the Lord. My sister has demonstrated humility and honesty by looking inward towards herself, as she crafted a book, that if read, will help many in the church achieve the Lord's Will for their marriages and professional lives.

Rev. Dr. Leo Daniel Jeffero, Jr., Th.D., MC, LMFT

Preface

The Word of God in the Book of 1 Corinthians 7:33-35

But he that is married careth for the things that are of the world, how he may please his wife. **34** There is difference also between a wife and a virgin. The unmarried woman careth for the things of the Lord, that she may be holy both in body and in spirit: but she that is married careth for the things of the world, how she may please her husband. **35** And this I speak for your own profit; not that I may cast a snare upon you, but for that which is comely, and that ye may attend upon the Lord without distraction.

This book will take you on a journey from my humble beginning to my present. It is a journal chronicling my life and how we can lose focus of what is important in our lives. This book will give you insight into my life as it relates to what I experienced in my childhood, adulthood, marriages and ministry.

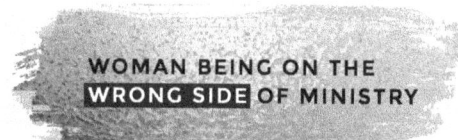

I will share with you my rich foundation of family love, family wisdom, and family work ethics. I will also share with you my fears, my pain, my anger, and my regrets at letting my flesh get the advantage over my spirit. Because of the betrayal I suffered, the respect and disrespect that was given, the deception and lies that were told, the lust and love that was deceptive, and my recovery and deliverance from it all; as I severed my marriage vows from my husband Jack.

I was an out of control, stressed-out, angry wife, mother, and First Lady, as I had lost my identity as the Godly woman God had called me to be. This book will expose all my hidden emotions, anger, and fears that I experienced from my childhood to my adulthood that led to the destruction of my family and my marriage.

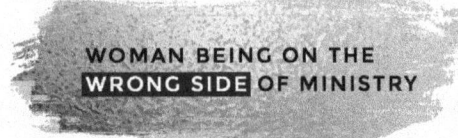

I will share with you all of my hidden emotions of anger and fears that were rooted deep within me.

I had to come face to face with myself and deal with the enemy that was within me.

I thank My Lord and Savior Jesus Christ for trusting me to carry and give birth to this book that is full of questions of Why Me? I know I am not the only one who has asked that question, there are many more "Why Me's" out there.

I also want to thank Dr. Fred Jones (My Book Coach) for all your expert advice, training courses and clients care calls.

It has been a pleasure being one of your clients.

I pray that this book will begin to help you deal with your individual issues and discover that you are chosen by God to tell your testimony and share your story to all that will take the time to listen with their heart and their ears.

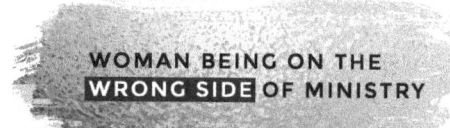

Introduction

It is amazing to me to be here actually writing this book about my journey through life thus far.

I never thought I was gifted or good enough to write my life story as it was unfolding right in front of my very eyes. To my amazement, God had given me a passion to pursue writing a book in the latter part of 2016. I thought this would be great for the women's ministry at our local church. I was getting so excited as I was planning for our first women's meeting in January of 2017. I was so excited about that first meeting, and the thought of sharing with the women's ministry my desire to write a book, and to encourage them to pray about writing a book as well.

I knew early in ministry that I was called to mentor and encourage women to not only give birth to their God given potential, but to know their worth in the Kingdom of God. I was always hungry for the presence and the movement of God amongst His people, so you can imagine my excitement about this book.

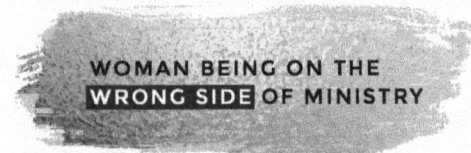

When God gave me the desire to write, I had no idea what kind of book I would write or the audience of readers I would be addressing... all I knew was that I had a desire to write a book. So, I began to seek out information about book writing and authors that have written books that not only inspired me, but also captivated me by their ability to not only write but to inspire their readers to continue to turn every page.

I found a tutorial video teaching of a very profound Man of great wisdom and knowledge who has always inspired and captivated his audience as he traveled around the world ministering the Gospel of Jesus Christ.

The late Dr. Myles Munroe's tutorial video teaching stirred up a desire in my Spirit that led me to write down some key points about writing. He was stimulating an appetite within me that I had a story to tell and that the only reason the world does not know my story is because I have not written it in a book so that the world would know my story....

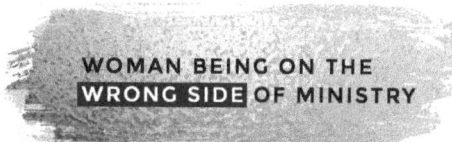

At this point I am blown away! How hard can it be to tell my story? I thought to myself as my zeal to write a book was being intensified even more with the feeling that I could write a book. But there was one thing the late Dr. Myles Munroe said that would be the defining difference, and would eventually confirm or deny me ever believing that I was qualified to write a book, and inspire its readers to turn each page. What was that comment the late Dr. Miles Monroe shared that really got me to search deep within myself to know beyond any doubt that I am transparent enough to not only write this book, but that I'm qualified to write it, because it is My Journey, My Testimony and My Deliverance! The defining quote that the late Dr. Munroe shared was:

"The only way you can write your story, is that you first must be an overcomer of what you are writing about."

At that point, I began to search my heart for confirmation from within that I was indeed qualified to tell my story.

It didn't take long for me to realize that I was not ready to share with the world my journey as it relates to being a wife to a Husband / Pastor, and me being a First Lady / Executive Pastor, a Teacher, Mentor, and Church Mother to an amazing church, not to mention a role model to our local community. The desire to write was beginning to be less desirable to me as I considered the repercussions I would face from my husband, children, family, and friends. I thought deeply about how they would feel about me exposing certain aspects of events that had happened in my life that I know had shaped me into this amazing woman that God has inspired to tell her story to all who will hear.

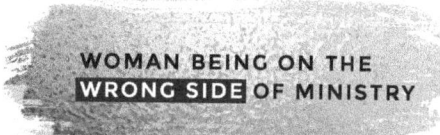

So, through many trials and tribulations, heartache and pain, misunderstanding, rejection, lies, resentment, anger, and feelings of despair, thoughts of not being good enough to the point of taking my own life, yes, you heard me right... I would have never thought being married to a pastor and serving in ministry together since the foundation of our church in October of 1997, that my marriage would be tested to the point of affairs that would lead to divorce... never in my thought process would I have ever imagined that the enemy would have destroyed my marriage of 34 plus years!!! So, come join me on My Journey as I share with you: "Being on The Wrong Side of Ministry". A Diary of an Ex Pastor's Wife.

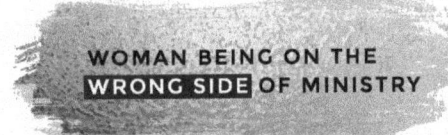

Copyright
Dedication
Foreword
Preface
Introduction
Table of Contents
Chapter

1.	In the Beginning I Was Born	The Chronicle of My Life
2.	Building A Foundation	Wrong Building Blocks
3.	Who Left the Door Open?	What Entered My Mind
4.	Maturing in What?	It is in My DNA
5.	The Growth Process	What Is Growing in Me?
6.	Change or No Change	Dealing with The Outer Me
7.	The Encounter	Meeting Jesus On My Skid Row
8.	The Call	Is It Godly or Is It You?
9.	My Way or God's Word	Not My Will
10.	Being on The Wrong Side of Ministry	Working for the Wrong Master
11.	Where Did It Fall Off At?	Was Blind, But Now I See
12.	The Conclusion	Doing the Word

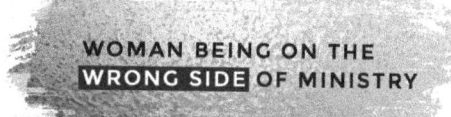

Chapter 1
In the Beginning
THE CHRONICLE OF MY LIFE

Philippians 1:6

Being confident of this very thing, that he which hath begun a good work in you will perform it until the day of Jesus Christ:

Where do I start: to connect the fibers of my genesis? Well for me that was easy, I went to the source of my very being...my mom. As I sat in my mom's comfy chair looking into her eyes that hold the wisdom of the wise, I took out my notepad, preparing to write. I then began to ask my mom several questions about me. She of course would look at me and smile as she began describing to me the day she went into labor with me. It was June 21, 1959 and it was an extremely hot day in Jacksonville, Florida, already almost 80 degrees before nine in the morning. My mother said she was doing her daily routine after my father had left for work, caring for my older siblings, when suddenly her water broke. She said back in those days you didn't leave right away to the hospital, so she started cleaning and cooking while having mild contractions. She made sure that my siblings at home had prepared food and clothing before leaving to give birth to me.

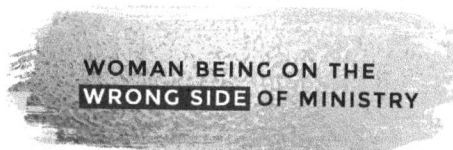

About 5:30 that afternoon, my mom fed my siblings and ate dinner herself because she knew once she got to the hospital, they were not going to feed her until after my birth. She then went to await my arrival. My mom said she was in hard labor with me until shortly after midnight on June 22, 1959, then I was finally born. The doctor said... It's a girl... hey y'all that was me coming into the world.

I weighed in at 7lb 4oz, sibling number six. Later, about six weeks after I was born, my mom's friend Miss Emma was visiting her. She was holding me when I briefly opened my eyes, and to her amazement, she said to my mother, "Clara, this baby has funny colored eyes. They look like they are blue." My mom pried open my eyes, and to her amazement, she confirmed that my eyes were indeed blue.

Childhood

When I asked my mother questions about my childhood, I was very curious to hear what she had to say about me, and I was really pleased to hear her say that I was a particularly good child, and that I was no trouble at all.

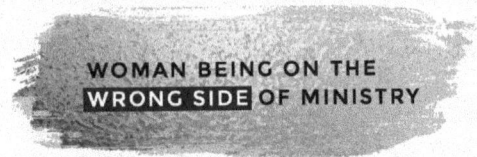

I was in shock!

I just assumed that I was a disappointment to her, but to hear her say I was a good child released me from being so judgmental of myself. While attending school in Hampton County at age seven, I was diagnosed with a hearing loss in my right ear. Being young, I did not realize the seriousness of my diagnosis. My mother did everything to assure that I would have a normal childhood. There were many doctors' appointments, hearing tests, surgeries, and more tests. I remember seeing those long white doctors' coats and thinking no, not again.

If I thought I could have just said no and that would be the end, I would have said no many years ago during those long trips to Charleston, S.C. All my test results showed permanent hearing loss with no signs of correction. So, I've learned to live with this diagnosis and at a young age learned to read lips to keep from having to say I didn't hear you, or back in those days, huh... which I got teased about a lot by family and friends to the point that I would start to pretend to hear and agree with whatever was said in fear of being reprimanded for something over which I had no control.

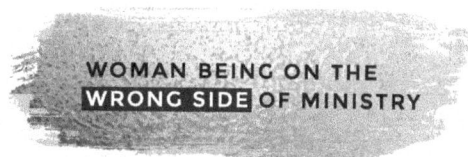

As I grew into my teenage years, I would experience other challenges as my mind and body were changing.

Adolescence

As a young girl, I always liked to work. I grew up raking yards, shelling butter beans and field peas, feeding the hogs, cleaning and washing dishes, helping my grandfather plant his gardens, and helping him fix his car under the big oak tree in the front yard. My grandfather was known as the tree shade mechanic and we all assisted him when needed. My grandfather raised all his grands to be a jack of all trades as he would say, so I know a little bit of everything, or I know how to figure it out...I call that Grandfather Wisdom. My mother also shared with me how helpful I was in aiding her with chores around the house. I have always liked to work and will help anyone with whatever they needed. Sometimes, that can be a blessing or a curse depending on the person. I became somewhat popular in high school and I had and still have a BFF (Teresa Greene Adams), to this day we are still the best of friends.

She is definitely my sister and we share a lot of advice with one another. She had book sense and I had common sense, but as we matured, she has outgrown me in common sense as well. I was exposed to a lot in my teenage years. I worked at a department store; I won a beauty pageant; I was a high school class officer, high school color guard, and yes, a proud high school graduate of the class of 1977. Little did I know that the next chapters of my life would take me on a journey for which I would have to chart out the course of direction, and what it would take to overcome the challenges that were already predestined for my life.

Adulthood

After graduating from high school, it didn't take me long to jump right into motherhood. I gave birth to a handsome baby boy that same year. About three weeks later, I married his father. At that time, I thought that was the right thing to do. I was raised without my father and I didn't want that for my son.

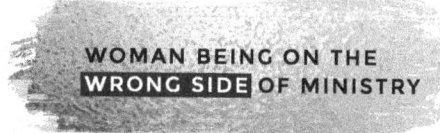

My husband at that time was a very jealous man. For the life of me, I don't know why I rushed to marry him knowing he was capable of causing me harm. I was somewhat afraid of him. It rained what they would say cats and dogs the day I got married...the older, wiser family members looked at that as a bad sign and it proved to be true. In October of 1979, I gave birth to our second son. After five years of what I call an abusive, controlling marriage, I left my sons' father. I felt like I was his child and not his wife and I could no longer subject our two sons to that behavior or that lifestyle, so I was legally separated from him in September of 1982 and we divorced in April of 1983.

The Encounter

Living in Hinesville, Georgia, I met a young man (who I will refer to as Jack throughout the chapters of this book) at the movies in 1982. Legally separated from my sons' father, I took my boys to the movies with my last five dollars. *Star Trek: The Wrath of Khan* was playing.

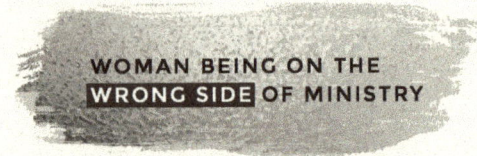

I just wanted to get a breath of fresh air, take my children and enjoy an evening out, not knowing the outcome of that day. The weather was very pleasant, not too hot with a light mid-September breeze. The line for the movies was getting longer as it was extending around the side of the building. While waiting in the long line, I noticed a young man walking and looking directly at me. I smiled and quickly looked away as he passed by me to stand in line. From my peripheral vision, I could see a shadow looking in my direction. Who is this man that kept staring at me? We were finally inside the theater after standing in that long line. I had to be very careful of my seating arrangement just in case my sons became restless or whiny, so I sat in the very last row of the theater. I could sense that someone was standing directly behind me, and there he was, again standing in the door while I was laughing to myself. He approached me: "Excuse me, Miss. Is this seat taken?" I looked and said "No, I do not think so." He replied, "You mind if I sit here?" My reply: "Sure, it is a free country." As he was sitting, he began to speak more and I noticed an accent, so I inquired, "Where are you from?" His reply: "Brooklyn, New York."

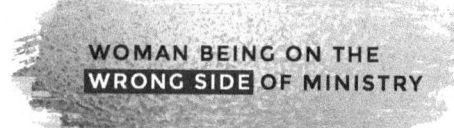

I thought to myself oh no... My mom told me to beware of those New York City slickers. I could no longer hear what he was saying...fear was beginning to grab my heart, trying to tune him out. I started talking to my sons. Then he said, "I'm going to the concession stand, do you want anything to eat?" I quickly said no. "What about your boys?" he asked. "Do they want anything?"

I took one look at my sons and, feeling very sad, knowing that they were hungry, I said, "Yes, you can bring them something." To my amazement he returned with a tray full of everything that they had at the concession. My heart melted. Who is this guy? Little did I know that meeting Jack that day at the movies would lead to the most awesome love affair I had ever experienced.

The Courtship

I will never forget that day in September 1982, the day I met this amazing man. Jack was the perfect gentleman, very courteous and polite, and he spoke well. To look at him, you would have never thought that he was a very knowledgeable young black man. To this day,
I really cannot say a whole lot about that movie because we talked through the entire movie.

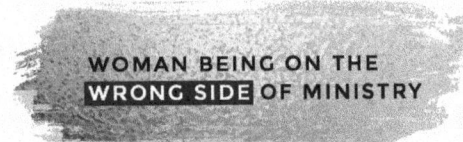

Jack was a U.S. Army Soldier and had just arrived days earlier to Fort Stewart, Georgia from Schweinfurt, Germany. I wasn't sure I was ready or wanted to pursue a relationship, just having separated from my sons' father. After the movies that evening, Jack accompanied me back to my apartment complex. I went upstairs, put my boys inside, and stood in my door talking, not inviting him into my apartment at all. Then Jack said, "I would like to see you again, would you like to go bowling with me tomorrow, that is if you are free?" And, of course, before I knew it, I said, "Would you like to come in?" I think that was the best decision I made that night. I asked him to excuse me while I prepared my sons for bed. When I returned, he was sitting there on the couch with his arm on the back and legs crossed. Listen to this, he was wearing cut-off jeans shorts with tube socks, shower shoes and a wife beater t-shirt. This is how he was dressed the first time we met. We spent that evening sharing our life stories of different things we had experienced.

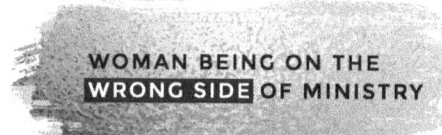

The Conversation

We talked for hours, as we were so engaged in conversation. The time was well spent. We shared our life experiences and our plans for future endeavors.

Wow, what a night that turned out to be. Jack was such a talker and very smart. He knew a little bit about everything, and he enlightened me on things that I didn't know. As the hour was getting late, we made arrangements to go bowling the next day. After saying our goodbyes that night, I went to bed and, for the first time since my separation, I felt like I could trust Jack with my heart to go on a bowling date. Ok... I know what you all are thinking, and I am thinking the same thing... I have not healed or given myself the time to heal and to learn to live with my own self and my two sons, and here I am leaping into another relationship. My mind raced all night long with questions: Who is this guy that is so engaged, kind, and gentle, painting a picture of the ideal guy I dreamed about and envisioned to be my husband?

Could God be sending me a good man that will love me and not abuse me? Wow! Even though I had just met him, it seemed as though I have known him all my life.

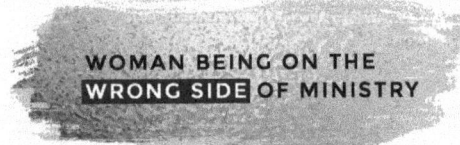

The First Date

So, the next day Jack arrived to take me bowling. One of my neighbors that I had known prior to moving had a teenage daughter that would babysit the boys for me. I was excited about getting a little alone time with someone that didn't remind me of my first failed marriage. I have also always liked bowling. I bowled on women's leagues as a stress relief, but my sons' father had shattered all the joy I had for bowling due to his extremely jealous nature. I began to live a life of fear.

Fear had entered my mind and I never knew when that man would freak out and just do awful things to me and my sons. That night, as I began to bowl, fear began to grip my heart again. I kept telling myself that he was gone, that he was not there, but as I prepared to release the ball, while fighting with the fear in my mind, I rolled the ball across my shoulder, hitting very few pins. I was so embarrassed to hit so few pins but, to my amazement, I got a pat on my derrière and a kiss on my cheek. Wow, I thought, I would just keep throwing across my shoulder if my reward was going to be so loving, thoughtful, and caring. Jack's affection for me just warmed my heart to the point that I was so in awe of his charm.

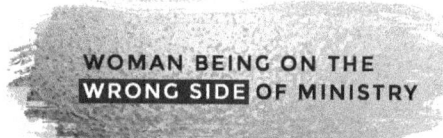

After our evening of bowling, we took a cab back to my apartment, where we spent some time sharing more about our life stories. I didn't have very much to offer him as refreshments while we shared our conversation, and after some time Jack left to return to the barracks. That night, I again tossed and turned, wondering, "Who is this guy?" He was like my knight in shining armor that came to rescue me from a heartbreaking five-year long devastating marriage.

My Confirmation

The next day, I took my five-year-old son to school and my three-year-old son was at home with me. I returned to do my daily chores of cooking, cleaning and laundry while my youngest played in his room or watched cartoons. It was a very pleasant day. That time of year, I always opened the windows to air out the house while I cleaned and did laundry. While in my living room dusting, I heard a car horn blowing. Looking out the window to see who it was, I saw him (Jack) standing outside the cab looking up at my window asking, "Are you dressed?" Of course, I said yes. He asked me to come down.

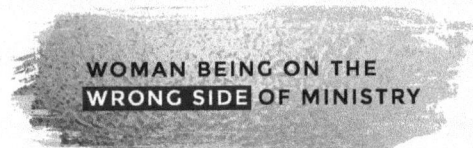

I asked, "Where we were going?" and he said that he was going to take me somewhere, so I grabbed my son and we proceeded to go downstairs to meet him. He said to get in and I asked again where we were going. He replied that he would tell me when I got in. To my amazement, he told the cab driver to take us to the commissary. My heart melted as I gazed into his eyes. He said that he had noticed when he was at my house yesterday that I did not have any food so he was taking me shopping to get food for me and my sons.

I was blown away and scared, as I could hear my mother's voice again in my ears saying not to let a man spend their money on you because then they will think they can control you. Oh my God, I was scared but I needed food for my sons...Lord help me! As we went into the commissary, he pulled out a cart, pointed to me and said to get what I needed and that he was going to pay for it. Can you hear me screaming inside? I wanted to cry, I wanted to hug him. Who is this guy? After drowning out the voice of my mother in my head, I proceeded to pick up items that I needed to feed my sons.

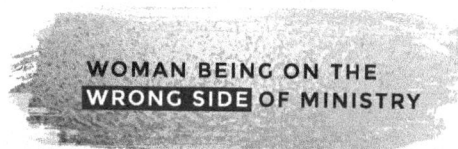

WOMAN BEING ON THE WRONG SIDE OF MINISTRY

I was forever humble and grateful and scared at the thought that this gentleman was caring enough to care for the needs of me and my sons. To show my appreciation to him for buying food for my household, I invited him over for a home-cooked meal. I prepared it with a lot of love, I remember laying a fake red rose beside his plate, giving him a kiss and saying thank you for caring.

The best thing about meeting this gentleman was that he was a great talker and I was a great listener. As we talked, we were connecting in conversation and compatibility on a level that was out of this world. Every time I was in his presence, I was intertwined with his world and I can imagine he felt the same way about me. Later that week, he came over and took me and my sons walking to the shopping center. It was not far from my apartment complex, so I had my youngest son by the hand and he had my oldest son by the hand as we were walking. Upon arrival, he took me into the shoe store. When the salesman asked if he could help us, he said that he would like to look for boy's sneakers.

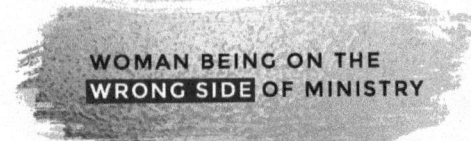

WOMAN BEING ON THE WRONG SIDE OF MINISTRY

My mouth dropped wide open. What!!! Who is this guy? Looking at me, he asked what size sneakers my sons wore. I was still in shock. Was I really hearing this? Now he wants to buy my boys some sneakers!!! Oh, this is too much, this is way too much. I don't know what to say... should I tell him their shoe size or should I refuse? After looking at me for a response, he realized that I was in shock, so he asked for a foot measurement scale and he measured both of my sons' feet. I was still in shock as he went to the shoe rack, began to pick out sneakers and had my sons try them on. After making a selection, he paid for them, put the old sneakers in the shoe box and, upon leaving the store, he threw them in the trash.

He impressed me with his thoughtfulness and generosity, but I had seen this kind of gesture before from my sons' father, who had also started out being very generous to me. In my mind, I began to reflect back on my experience from dating and marrying my sons' father.

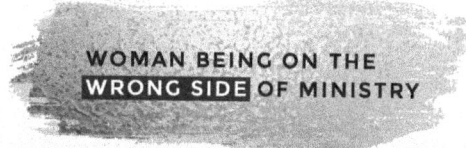

WOMAN BEING ON THE WRONG SIDE OF MINISTRY

Chapter 2
Building A Foundation

WRONG BUILDING BLOCKS

1 Corinthians 3:10

According to the grace of God which is given unto me, as a wise masterbuilder, I have laid the foundation, and another buildeth thereon. But let every man take heed how he buildeth thereupon.

It was the summer of 1975 when I met my sons' father. We both grew up in the same little town in the country. We would meet up at softball games back in those days. We started out just sharing small talk, nothing serious. We would walk to each other's houses. We rode the same school bus. After some time, we became very fond of each other. We began what we called back in those days courting each other. In my early childhood, I was brought up in a strict home environment and my main goal was to finish school, go to college, get married and have a family... funny how things do not work out completely the way we envision them.

In the summer of 1976, I competed in an African American beauty pageant. The sponsors of the beauty pageant had convinced my mother that I had a good chance of winning, so my mother consented to them working with me on the requirements necessary to compete.

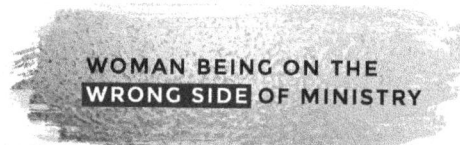

I had to work hard that summer getting business ads for the souvenir booklet. I also hosted a dance event to raise money for charities, while also attending pageant rehearsals for the talent competition, question and answer competition and evening gown competition. The pageant was in the early part of June. I was getting nervous about that pageant and each day leading to the competition was causing my heart to race faster and faster. Finally, it was the night that would decide the winner of the Miss Bronze Hampton County Beauty Pageant. In those days, we used a record player with the forty-five records in which you had to insert a tab in the open hole before playing. I remember I was on the stage ready to do the talent competition and the record player needle kept skipping through the entire song. I started to just give up, but I'm not a quitter, so, as scared and embarrassed as I was, I followed through with my talent presentation. In spite of all of that, I won the beauty contest. I was very shocked! I walked out on that stage and was crowned Miss Bronze Hampton County. As I reflected back on that amazing day, I look at what I accomplished by winning that pageant. I was given a crown, a partial scholarship toward college, and I attended a lot of special events as Miss Bronze Hampton County.

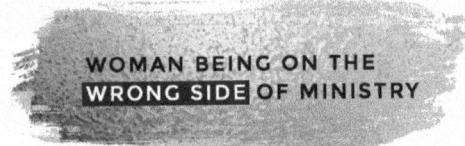

As I entered my senior year of high school, I was still dating my son's father. He drove the school bus because he was a senior and had a license in good standing, and of course I rode his bus. Every month when he got paid, he would buy me stuff. Back in those days, having money at that age, while still in school, seemed to be a lot. I was spending a lot of time with him, being with him had become the norm for me. We were what you would call going steady. My mother, on the other hand, was still very strict and did not understand that I was in what I called love at that time. In the early part of the school year, I found out that I was pregnant. I just knew that my mother was going to kill me! She was disappointed of course, and I did not consider what it meant to be pregnant. I just knew that I was in love.

At that age, I never considered what I was giving up until I was faced with the fact that I would still be required to finish school. I had to surrender my crown from winning Miss Bronze Hampton County 1976, and with that I lost a partial scholarship to college along with all of the upcoming events where I would have represented my hometown of Hampton County, South Carolina.

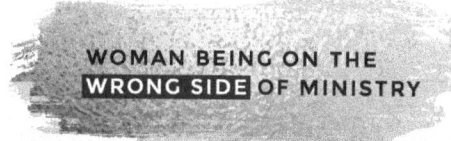

WOMAN BEING ON THE WRONG SIDE OF MINISTRY

I felt bad and I was embarrassed for my actions, but I held my head up high, completed high school and yes, I marched across that stage and received my high school diploma on May 30, 1977. I gave birth to my first son on June 10, 1977. I don't consider my first born to be a mistake, he was and still is my first blessing.

Later that month, I married my son's father on June 25, 1977. I felt that it was the right thing to do, knowing my family tradition that they did not believe in having a baby out of wedlock. Even though I got married after having my son, I was still required to go before the church and ask for forgiveness. I did it not fully understanding why, but I did it. My son's father then joined the military to provide for my son and I. After basic training, he was assigned to Fort Bliss, Texas. My son and I eventually joined him in Texas, but it was not a very happy marriage. We had a lot of problems. My son's father was jealous and abusive at times, physically, mentally and verbally. We had a lot of money problems, as he did not make a lot of money back in those days, and sometimes his drinking influenced the abuse. I was living a life of fear. I did everything to assure him that we were good.

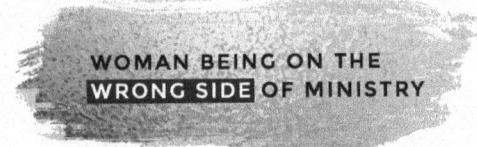

Being a young married wife at eighteen, moving away from family to a state that I had never been to before, and raising a son while living in that abusive environment was beginning to drain me emotionally, eventually leading to anxiety, fear and depression.
I was emotionally, mentally and physically abused... my heart was in pieces. Afraid to share this with my family, I kept it to myself. This was the start of an open door to spousal abuse. How did I get here?... I would ponder in my mind. I tried everything to convince him that I loved him, but no amount of persuasion was working. I began to isolate myself from our neighbors, not opening the door or opening the windows. I felt trapped. Not wanting to return to my mother's house, I continued to take the abuse. I was convinced that I was a failure, not capable of being a good wife. My fairytale dream of a happy marriage was not going to happen. Little did I know what was in store for me as my journey continued.

All of this was replaying in my mind as I was shoe shopping with this new man. I know what you are thinking as I was thinking the same thing. He cannot be real...it is not going to last.

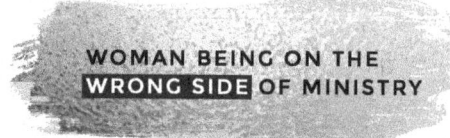

WOMAN BEING ON THE WRONG SIDE OF MINISTRY

I am going to be let down again, but I was so drawn to his gentle spirit, compassionate heart and generosity towards me and my sons when I needed help. My heart was leading me where my mind did not want to go.

As we held hands walking back to the apartments with the boys walking on each side, in my mind I felt fear, but in my heart, I felt love. I desperately needed something drastic to happen before this gentleman captured my heart.

I did not have a relationship with God back then as I do now, but I was reaching toward God for a sign before I invested my time, my heart and my kids' hearts too. Walking home, I was amazed and awestruck.
I continued to ask him questions hoping for one wrong answer, but he had none. He was very smart, a little too smart for me. That was my fear, that he has been around and had been exposed to more than I have ever seen. I'm just a country girl from South Carolina and he is a New York City slicker, as my mother would say. But I could not deny that we had great chemistry in communication and our hearts were beginning to trust that what we were feeling was real.

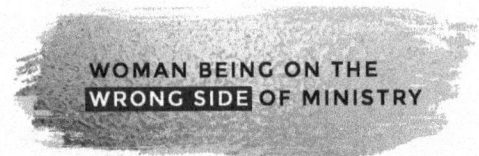

As you can see, my life had taken a turn to what I felt was the right direction but fear still lurked around the corner. I really wanted to believe that this was the right thing to do, pursuing a relationship with this young man even though I'm recently legally separated, feeling abandoned, having been punished and abused by my sons' father. There was still a sense of loneliness and wanting to belong to someone. I felt like I had failed at marriage. I felt very ashamed, knowing the background, culture, and traditions of my family. I knew what they believed as it pertains to marriage: one husband and one wife. I felt trapped in a hopeless situation, believing that I would have to live the rest of my life without a husband or a father for my two young sons. As I pondered this in my heart, I felt more ashamed of my present situation. I felt like Paul in the Bible when he said I was be-twitch between two.

The next day as we talked about it, I shared with Jack that I felt convicted and condemned. Jack tried to reassure me through scripture that God would not condemn me because I had a failed marriage.

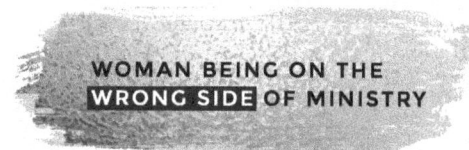

Of course, I thought he was just saying something to reassure me and calm me down, but I have come to realize that God does love me, that He is concerned about everything that concerns me and that he does not hold me accountable for my failed marriage. The Bible holds man accountable as the head of the household and the man covers his wife and his children.

Never allow anyone to plant fables in your mind as I did. Build yourself up on rightly dividing the Word of God, for His Word is proven to be a sure foundation!

1 Corinthians 11:3 But I would have you know, that the head of every man is Christ; and the head of the woman is the man; and the head of Christ is God.

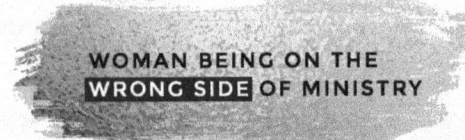

Chapter 3
Who Left the Door Open?
WHAT ENTERED MY MIND

James 4:7

Submit yourselves, then, to God. Resist the devil, and he will flee from you.

An open door can allow someone or something to enter our space, sometimes willingly, sometimes unwillingly. The very essence of thoughts entering our mind can and will affect our emotional state of being.

I can remember growing up in South Carolina as a young girl, living with my grandparents in a big wood slant house on the side of Highway 68. There was a huge oak tree on the side of the house that provided shade on hot summer days. Closer to the highway were two smaller trees with a bench between them for sitting. We always played under that big oak tree, my grandmother and her sisters would shell butter beans and field peas under that oak tree also, and my grandfather would fix cars under it. Family and friends knew him as the tree shade mechanic.

My grandmother was always inside doing chores around the house and preparing meals for the family.

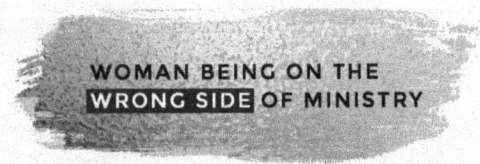

I can still to this day hear my grandmother asking who had left the screen door open. Back in those days, my grandparents were farmers who raised livestock...hogs and chickens.

The chickens were free to roam the yard, so we called them yard chickens. Sometimes as children we would forget and leave the screen door open after entering or leaving the house and the smallest opening was enough for a chicken to enter. They would then eat whatever was in sight until my grandmother would chase them out with her straw broom and latch the screen door. Similarly, it is amazing how we at times allow thoughts to enter the door to our mind, and instead of casting them down as the scripture said, we just allow those thoughts to enter in and we start entertaining them.

2 Corinthians 10:5 Casting down imaginations, and every high thing that exalteth itself against the knowledge of God, and bringing into captivity every thought to the obedience of Christ.

While I lived with my grandparents in South Carolina, I always liked being in what my grandmother would call *"grown folks' conversation"*.

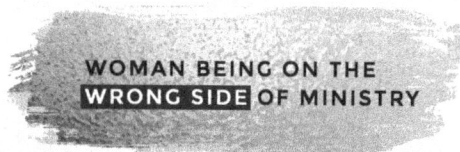

As a young girl, I was always around my grandmother and her sisters or her sisters-in-law. As they were talking, I was always listening. I enjoyed some of the conversations they shared, some would linger in my mind longer than others. I know now that some of the thoughts that lingered from those conversations
helped shape my life. Whether they were good or bad, I had to deal with those thoughts as I grew into my adult life. As I reflect back, I can remember listening to some conversations that would literally scare me to the point of not wanting to sleep by myself, and then there were those conversations that would frighten me to the point that I would not walk by myself after dark.

What was entering my mind was the spirit of fear. I had fear to the point of anxiety. Hyperventilating and gasping for air, I would break out in a cold sweat and at times it felt like my entire body was paralyzed and my speech frozen. That was the beginning of an open door for fear to enter my mind.

As a teenager, my anxiety and fear intensified. It was tormenting me. I would ask my siblings to sleep with me.

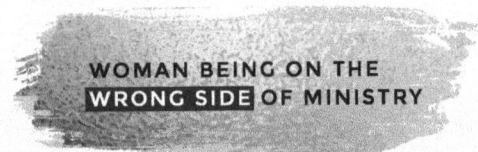

I started frequently wetting my bed because I was afraid of getting up at night. My heart would beat so fast I thought it would jump out of my chest. I was having nightmares about a little black creature chasing me. I would be running so fast in my dreams that I would just fly above them to escape. I can still remember waking up in a cold sweat gasping for air.

I remember going to the movies to watch The Exorcist. I was so scared when I got home, I begged my mother to let me sleep with her. I tell you that if my mother had not let me sleep with her, I'm not sure that I would have made it through that night. I was so glad that I was able to sleep with my mother. I felt safe and at peace sleeping with my mother that night.

As you can see, fear had taken me on a journey from a very young age, into my teenage years, young adult years, and into my adult years. Fear brought more anxiety and torment. The devil was trying to take my very life. Whatever unhealthy thoughts I allowed to enter my mind would continue to grow there, leaving me to explore or entertain those thoughts even while I was sleeping.

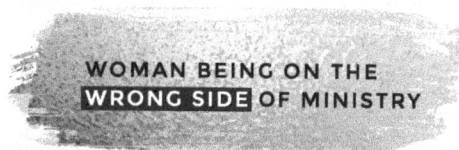

WOMAN BEING ON THE WRONG SIDE OF MINISTRY

Fear was tormenting me while I slept to the point that my dreams became nightmares. I was talking in my sleep and imagining the worst. This was my life growing up in South Carolina. Fear led me to alcohol and drug use. I was drinking early in my teenage years and then I started experimenting with marijuana and speed shortly after separating from my son's father. It was during this time that I met Jack.

We started dating in September of 1982 and we married the following year on June 4, 1983, and I gave birth to our son that following year in January of 1984. Jack had orders for a tour overseas and my son's and I would join him there in April of that same year. I continued using alcohol and drugs overseas to drown out fear. It wasn't until I committed my life to Christ that I was able to face all of my fears and be delivered from the clutches of the devil.

After committing my life to Christ and being saved for some months, I received the baptism of the Holy Spirit. It was then that the Lord began to reveal to me the attacks the enemy had planned for me when I was a young girl.

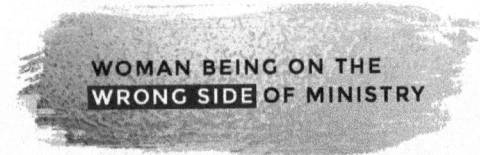

The fear that I experienced through my failed marriage, the old wives' fables, and nightmares was meant to drive me to take my own life. As one door of fear closed, another door of fear opened. Each door had its own level of torment, leaving me in such a state of anxiety to just end it all, that it took the Blood of Jesus to save me from all of my fears. Thank God for delivering me from the spirit of fear.

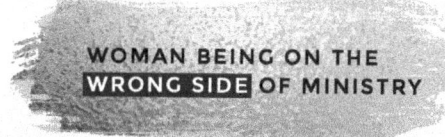

WOMAN BEING ON THE WRONG SIDE OF MINISTRY

Chapter 4
Maturing in What?
IT IS IN MY DNA

Jeremiah 1:4-5

Then the Word of the Lord came unto me, saying,

5 Before I formed thee in the belly I knew thee; and before thou camest forth out of the womb I sanctified thee, and I ordained thee a prophet unto the nations.

Have you ever been told that you look just like your mother or that you act just like your father? Well, join the DNA club. All of us at one time or another have been told that we are definitely our parents' child. Why? Because DNA does not lie.

As I began to look up the definition of DNA, it was very complex to me. I looked in DNA for Dummies and it defined DNA as an extremely long chain of molecules that contains all the information necessary for the life functions of a cell. DNA is the blueprint of our life, every cell in our body has DNA. After hearing this, I thought that I could not be anyone but Douglas & Clara Lee. I am nothing but a chain of D&C.

Regardless of whether or not I knew my parents, DNA is a sure way to connect the data through science to find out to whom I belong.

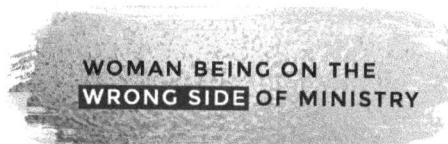

In my younger years, I was always told I acted just like my father. As I reflect back on the memories I have of my father, I remember him always as a very confident man, straightforward, firm but kind and loving. He was always telling stories and jokes to make people laugh. He was a tall, slim man and he walked with a swagger that fit his personality. People were always attracted to him and his outgoing personality. He was a vocal person. You would hear him before you saw him. He liked being the center of attention. His confident mindset always prevented him from being offended by others' expectations of him.

My mother always said that I was just like my dad, because she said that nothing or no one could hurt my feelings. Little did my mother know that I was always hurting and afraid because I did not think I fit in with most people. I used to get up and start doing chores around the house. I loved working. I would do whatever I could just to gain approval. I definitely have some of the same characteristics as my father: I'm good at guarding my emotions to protect my feelings. I will not say that I didn't get my feelings hurt sometimes, but what I will say is that I was very good at masking my true feelings in order to limit the effects of any insults.

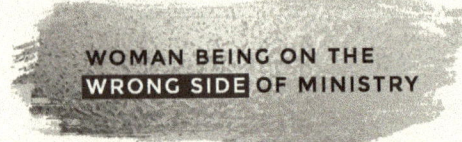

As I got older, I looked just like my mother, who we affectionately called granny. My mother was and still is an exceptionally beautiful, diligent woman that is full of wisdom and insight. She has a love for fashion and is a very stylish woman, even after having given birth to eight children. To look at her, you would never imagine the devastating pain and anguish that plagued her as she went from being married to being a single parent of seven children.

After my mother's failed marriage, we moved back to Camp Branch, South Carolina from Jacksonville, Florida. My grandparents opened their home to all seven of us. My mother was working two jobs to provide for us and help with the bills. I can remember seeing her leaving for work in the evening around five or six o'clock, walking to what was called a juke-joint back in the day. My mother always worried about providing for us. Sometimes I would see her crying about where our next meal was coming from or how she was going to provide clothing for us. We were outgrowing clothes faster than my mother's salary could replace them; there was never enough money to buy all of the necessary clothing.

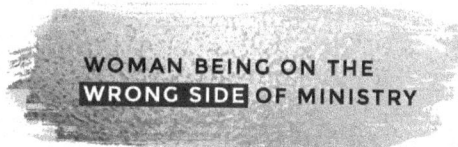

I believe that I patterned most of my adult life after my mom. I also believe that most of my mom's hurt, anger and pain from her failed marriage manifested in me, as I had witnessed her reactions of resentment, disappointment, anger, betrayal and pain. Little did I know that I was carrying the seeds of much of what my mother had suffered and endured in her marriage to my father. I remember when my dad came to visit in the summer of 1999. I was so glad to see my estranged father after all those years of not having a father present in my life. I was at my mother's house, and, like I said, my dad never met a stranger. He talked to everyone and that day he did just that and my mother was so mad. It was as if her past came back to remind her of how my father had disrespected her. At that point, my mother started fussing at him to the point of trying to control him. I was shocked at the way she was speaking to my father. I looked for a reaction or a reply, but my father just smiled as if he was used to it and said nothing. I realized at that point that my mom was still hurt, angry and bitter with my dad. It was as if she was back in Jacksonville, Florida, where my father left her on the street with seven children.

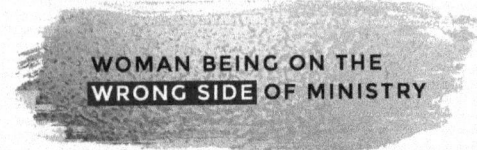

WOMAN BEING ON THE WRONG SIDE OF MINISTRY

She felt like he was still disrespecting her, flirting with other women. I have come to realize that most of my molecular DNA is my mother's. I was home for a family gathering in September of 2017 and I spent some time with my mom alone to share our similarities and personality. My mom and I have a way of settling conflicted issues that may come off as being a bit extreme at times. My mother, after discovering that my father came home with lipstick on his shirt collar, cooked hot tar to put on my dad's lips. My mother was not an evil person, but she despised liars and cheaters. She would cuss you out to beat the band. As you have probably figured out by now, I was the cussing one in the family, and I would bite and scratch you too, if I had to.

I can see how this DNA from my parents has shaped my life. Through the years, I have developed into almost a carbon copy of my mother. The fact of the matter is that you don't really see how some of the negatives of DNA will or has affected your life as you are growing into adulthood. I had been married to my husband at that time for thirty-three years.

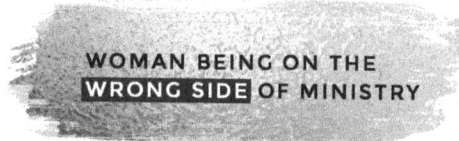

WOMAN BEING ON THE WRONG SIDE OF MINISTRY

In January of 2017, my marriage and my life took a turn that led to the separation of a godly marriage, so I thought. Jack and I were both going through a midlife crisis. I was prayerful and confident that the God that we served would be able to heal and restore everything according to his Word.

Chapter 5
The Growth Process

WHAT IS GROWING IN ME?

Matthew 12:33

Either make the tree good, and his fruit good; or else make the tree corrupt, and his fruit corrupt: for the tree is known by his fruit.

We believe that we are capable of sizing a person up just by looking at them, to the point of knowing whether they are happy or sad, rich or poor, healthy or sick, but just looking at the outward physical appearance of a person doesn't really tell you about their diet, personality, family life or fears. Some people can walk around us for days or years and we will never know their inward pain or insecurities; that will continue to grow within them daily as they continue to camouflage them with fake smiles and conversations. We may never realize that their pain or insecurities are growing more intense daily.

Ever since my childhood, I have always thought of myself as the black sheep of the family. I am sure that most of my siblings and other family members do not share this view of me, but this was my insecurity. I was my mother's sixth child, there were four sisters and one brother before me.

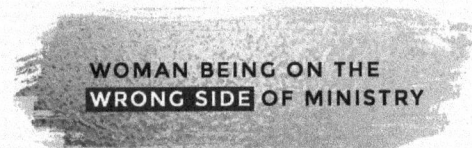

When I was born, my mother had no idea that I was born with blue eyes. My mother told me that I was about three weeks old when a friend of the family discovered that my eyes were blue. My mother shared with me that while she was in labor, I was accidentally poked in my eye by the attending nurse, so when I was born, my eye was bloodshot. She was given drops to put in my eyes to prevent infection. My mother said that it was hard for her to get the drops in, as I barely opened my eyes, so she couldn't believe it when she saw them. As to my mother's account as to how I happened to be born with blue eyes, she will tell you it's because of a black blue-eyed doll that she wanted for my older sisters. She could not afford to buy it for them, so she would go to that store every day and just look at the dolls in the window, until one day my father caught her there and told her to go home. My mother said she cried for days about those dolls while she was pregnant with me, so God blessed her with me, her blue-eyed doll-baby.

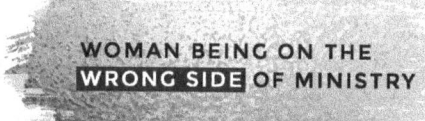

I was what my mom would call the knee baby because I was the baby twice because my brother that was born after me only lived for six weeks and returned to heaven. My mother said that a lot of people thought that I was an outside child, or the milkman's baby, but I will tell you that I am my father's child. My mother would often say to me that you are just like your father. My mother said that when I was a toddler, my dad would have her dress me up so he could take me with him to show me off to his friends. Listening to my mother talking about it, I don't think she was too happy about some of the places or houses that my father was visiting with me. I cannot remember anything about those days because I was just a toddler, I am just sharing what my mom shared with me.

I have always struggled with fear and feelings of insecurity. I was a very skinny teenager and I was slowly developing into a young lady. I remember seeing girls my age growing into young ladies and wondering why it was taking so long for me. I was an extremely late bloomer. I was often told that I was not my mother's daughter.

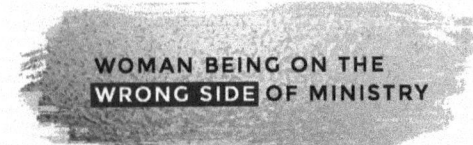

Most of my sisters were very blessed, I guess they had a brick house and I just had a brick. I always felt that my so-called friends were ridiculing me, to the point of feeling as if I was not good enough to hang out with them. I just wanted to isolate myself from people, feeling more and more like the odd one or a misfit. I never wanted to wear clothes that were very fitting to the body as I felt that others would be laughing at me behind my back. My level of insecurity was really controlling my young life.

Growing up, I was always referred to as Clara Lee's blue-eyed baby. To this day, I never could see what the big deal was about my eyes. I used to hate the fact that I had them. I felt like I suffered from a lot of hate because of them. The insecurity and pain that was growing inside of me was a result of what we would call bullying today. Many of my family members never knew this about me until now, that is, if they are reading it in this book. I can now say that by the Grace of God I am delivered from my pain and insecurity. I know now that I was created in the image of God.

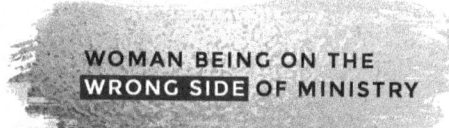

Psalm 139:14 I will praise thee; for I am fearfully and wonderfully made: marvelous are thy works; and that my soul knoweth right well.

I am so grateful to God that he protected me from myself and kept me in my youthful mindset that prevented me from trying to fit in with the wrong crowd that could have led me down the wrong road. Now, I do not want any of you to think that I was squeaky clean and sinless; no, I committed my share of sin. There were times that I wanted to fit in with the crowd to prevent them from picking on or mocking me, which would add to my pain and insecurity.

I had to learn to deal with what was growing inside of me. My family could not see it or even imagine that I was experiencing these insecurities. I had to go to God and seek Him for my deliverance. It was only after I cried out to God in prayer that I could see the evil that could have entrapped me, leading me into a lifestyle that would have hindered me from ever experiencing the Glory of God.

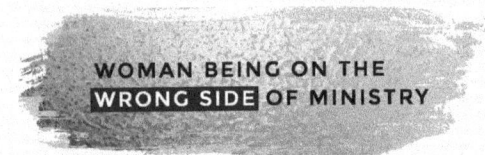

I want to encourage everyone who is reading this book to take this time to address all of the pain and insecurities that are growing inside of you and call them out, denounce their power of control over your mind and cast them out in Jesus' Name, Amen!

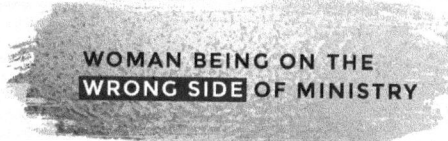

Chapter 6
Change or No Change
DEALING WITH THE OUTER ME

1 Peter 3:3

Whose adorning let it not be that outward adorning of plaiting the hair, and of wearing of gold, or of putting on of apparel; 4 But let it be the hidden man of the heart, in that which is not corruptible, even the ornament of a meek and quiet spirit, which is in the sight of God of great price.

K.I.S.S.... Keep It Simple Saints. This saying must have been lurking in the back of my mind. As far back as I can remember, I was never what you would call a fashion person. Simple has always worked for me.

My mother, on the other hand, has always worked hard to provide for all seven of us. She would use every means of credit to purchase clothes for us, even though we were what you would have described as below the poverty level. My mother would make sure that we dressed well: hair groomed, shoes shining with that royal crown hair grease and face greased down with royal crown hair grease as well.

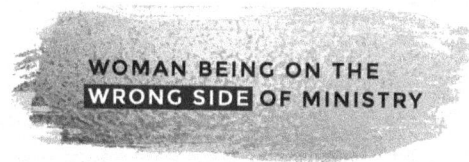

WOMAN BEING ON THE WRONG SIDE OF MINISTRY

Back in those days, money was hard to come by. In my teenage years, I took a home economics class that taught me a little about sewing, from cutting out a pattern to sewing it together. My mother would purchase fabric in many bright colors and my siblings and I were so excited to make our own clothing, whether all our notches were together or not.

As I was growing up, seeing how hard my mother worked to provide for us, I never wanted her to worry about me wanting to have certain clothing, so I was always grateful for what I had. I wasn't a fashion person then and, to this day, my sister Cynthia will remind me that I don't know how to dress. Her acknowledging it to me doesn't make me feel bad at all. Do not get me wrong, however, as I am a pretty decent dresser. I just don't always give a lot of attention to details and I also don't have a shoe fetish. All shoes, I don't care how cute they are, hurt my feet, so there you have it.

When my then husband Jack accepted his calling to preach the Word of God, I began to wonder if my style of dressing would be scrutinized by other ministers' wives.

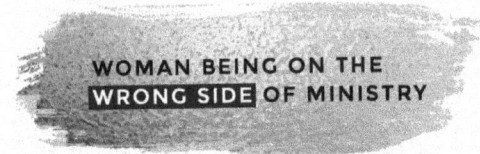

WOMAN BEING ON THE WRONG SIDE OF MINISTRY

Would I be asked to comply with the various dress codes pertaining to being a minister's wife? Of course, I didn't want to rebel against anything that would reflect back on Jack. I was taught and trained by the older women in the church to submit to those who had rule over you and to always govern yourself accordingly. So from wearing black and white on first Sundays, to all white on special occasions, hats, no makeup to makeup in moderation, to long dresses with church mothers measuring your hem, to wearing nail polish and large earrings. You name it, and I'm in there somewhere striving to abase and abound.

Whew... back then there were a lot of do's and don'ts. I'm amazed at myself when I reflect back on all that I did to make sure my outer appearance reflected what was required of me to validate myself as a submissive minister's wife. To all of the ladies looking to judge us or size us up by their standard, just a few words of wisdom and knowledge from a former pastor's wife: try praying for us more, and judging us less.

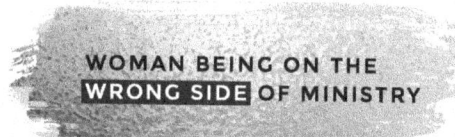

WOMAN BEING ON THE WRONG SIDE OF MINISTRY

Sometimes I think that members hold us to a higher standard, and they should rightfully expect us to represent the body of believers in every area of ministry. Trust me when I say this: I believe I speak for every pastor's wife that serves alongside her called husband when I say that we strive to lead and to set a good example of love, grace and kindness. It would be nice if we could get the same example from the body of believers as well.

As a mature, seasoned, ex-pastor's wife, I am extremely comfortable in my walk with the Lord. My outward appearance does have a part in it, but my focus and passion flows from the hidden man of my heart. I am at peace with my appearance and I am at peace knowing that God looks at the intent of our heart more than our garments. There is a wise saying that I have heard over the course of my life that says: Clothes do not make the person, the person wearing the clothes must have a heart that transcends the personality and character that reflects Christ.

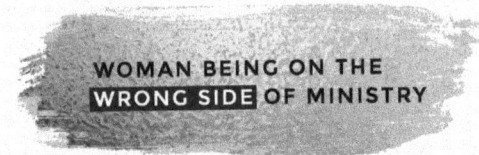

WOMAN BEING ON THE WRONG SIDE OF MINISTRY

Chapter 7
The Encounter

MEETING JESUS ON MY SKID ROW

Genesis 32:24-26

And Jacob was left alone; and there wrestled a man with him until the breaking of the day. **25** And when he saw that he prevailed not against him, he touched the hollow of his thigh; and the hollow of Jacob's thigh was out of joint, as he wrestled with him. **26** And he said, Let me go, for the day breaketh. And he said, I will not let thee go, except thou bless me.

As far back as I can remember, I was always what we would call a daydreamer. Living in Hampton County in a small community called Camp Branch, South Carolina on the roadside of Highway 68, one of my favorite sayings about choosing a house is that granddaddy raised me on the side of Highway 68 and that was as far into the woods as I would live. My mother had always worked several jobs in our younger years, so we were always at our grandparents' house. I can remember getting up early in the morning to my grandmother's southern breakfast cooking and the smell of coffee brewing.

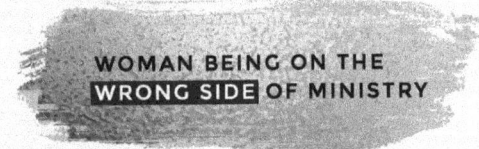

After she served my grandfather and us breakfast, she would always get herself a cup of coffee with cheese toast on her coffee saucer, her toast was always saturated with the overflow from the coffee in her cup.

After breakfast, we would go outside to play. On those long, hot summer days, I would always seek out the coolest spots while awaiting the cool southern breeze. Whether I was climbing up the pecan tree in the back yard or sitting under the big oak tree in the front yard, I would always find a spot where I could feel the cool breeze. It was at those times that I would escape in my mind and daydream about anything and everything that I wanted to do, build, or say. You name it, I was always daydreaming about it. I have always had big dreams pertaining to how I envisioned my life. I've had dreams about being a successful person and a humanitarian. If it involves helping, feeding, encouraging, empowering, equipping, sharing or mentoring, you can count me in.

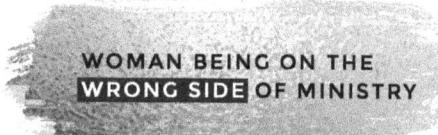

I was about seven years old when I was diagnosed with a hearing impairment in my right ear that was limiting my ability to understand in school and at home. My hearing loss was becoming very challenging. I also had a speech impediment that caused me to speak with a lisp. After I had been seen by numerous doctors, my mother realized that they were just using me for their experimental research, so she discontinued my visits.

From a young age, I was always a great talker. I had learned the art of conversation from a lineage of older women that I was privileged to sit with while they were shelling field peas and butter beans. They would always meet in the cool of the day under the big old oak tree to talk about whatever. I would always be close by listening in to their conversations and listening to them talk really helped me learn how to communicate about various subject matters. I loved being around grandmother (Lucille), her sister (Mamie), their sisters, and sisters in laws. I gleaned so much knowledge from all of them.

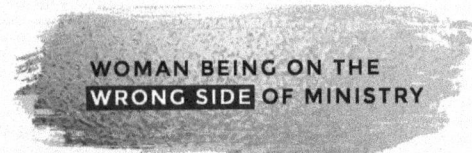

I don't know why, but I have always been attracted to older women's wisdom, knowledge and advice that was shared through conversations. I would listen to them talk about everything from A-Z. Yes, I was always in "their talk". It was easy for me because most of their meeting times would be when they were shelling butter beans or field peas and they liked me to hang around because I was fast at shelling beans and gathered the empty shells so that they would never have to get up.

I was told that my father was a great talker as well. I think I inherited a lot of his personality traits when it comes to talking, and my ability to hold a conversation, and even to defend myself against false accusations. Not only was I a talker, but I was also very outspoken. If something was missing, said or done, it was always my fault. Most of the time I was not aware of the situation but, because I thought I was grown, I talked like I was grown. It was always me that was going to get the switch... in other words a whipping.

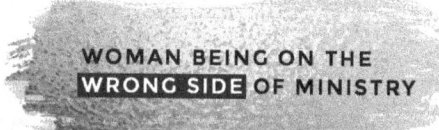

I was accused of stuff that I did not do, take, or say. My siblings sometimes would laugh at me and mock my pleading and crying. I would be angry to the point of wanting to hurt them for lying on me. I was accused of things that I had not done to the point that I started running from my whoopings down the dirt road from my grandfather's house. My mother sent my siblings after me, but I was running for my life and I was not letting any of them catch me.

In my adult life I am still faced with being falsely accused of things I did not do. Most of these accusations came from people I trusted, like my then husband Jack, my children and my close friends. About two plus years ago, I took a trip to Hawaii to visit my mentor and friend, Toni. I was in need of some mentorship / spiritual counseling and healing. My friend Toni was a gifted counselor even before getting her degree in counseling. She has always been able to talk me down or up, depending on my situation.

I was just at the beginning stage of my marriage crisis and I needed to talk with someone who would not sugar coat the Word of God, would give me Godly advice and would give me the truth as they perceived it pertaining to me. Toni had been in my life for over twenty plus years and has mentored me throughout. Toni was always able to get me to see myself, whether it was good or bad. This deliverance encounter would expose a side of me that I call "Meeting Jesus on My Skid Row."

I define "My Skid Row" as a desperately unfortunate or inconvenient situation.

While visiting with Toni, I was trying to figure out why my marriage was suffering from what I believed were fixable issues. For most of my young adult life, I couldn't see how I was trying to justify every accusation that was said about me, from Jack and my children down to a few of the brethren in the church, and to my surprise a few women too, that were taken in by the malicious lies being spread throughout our small community.

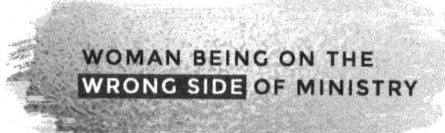

. was trying to defend myself against every accusation. I felt like no one was speaking up on my behalf, so I had to do It myself. My mentor Toni was driving me around Honolulu, Hawaii and the sights were breathtaking. Their plants are the greenest I've ever seen, and their beaches are the bluest I've ever seen. There is something about being near the water that calms and refreshes your Spirit.

It was in Hawaii that I was confronted with my skid row. It happened when my friend / mentor interrupted me as I was complaining once again about malicious lies that were being said about me. She asked me one question. She simply asked "Lin," as she affectionately calls me, "If you say you love God and trust Him with your life, then why are you always defending yourself against what people are saying about you?" At that moment, something broke in me and all I could do was cry. It was as if I was shattered into a thousand pieces. The tears continued to flow down my face and onto my chest. I felt numb and ashamed at the same time. Coming face to face with my skid row, I was speechless and too embarrassed to face my friend.

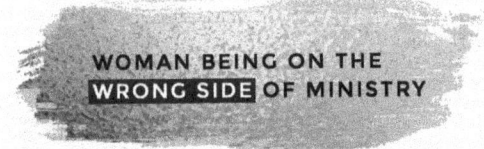

WOMAN BEING ON THE WRONG SIDE OF MINISTRY

The only words that were needed at that time were: Lord forgive me for not trusting you to fight all my battles.

I have come to realize that I am a whiner. My siblings would say that I'm a brat. I no longer defend myself against what they say. I will confess to them all that they are right and get myself some much-needed counseling. This was the beginning stage of my deliverance from trying to affirm myself to people who had formed an opinion about me through someone else's eyes.
I repented for doubting that God was able to defend me. As God continued to deliver me from myself, I could see situation after situation where I had denied God access to fight my battles for me. The more he showed me, the more I was broken. This process of deliverance in my walk with God is ongoing. I have to remind myself daily that this battle belongs to God. So, I am just like Jacob when he wrestled with the Angel until daybreak and wouldn't let him go until He Blessed Him, and not only did the Angel bless him, but he also changed his name.

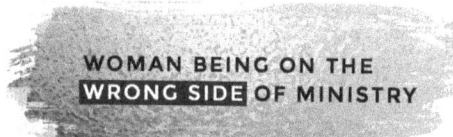

I no longer chase down, defend, or justify what is being said about me. Jesus met me at my place of desperation, brokenness, bitterness, anger and fear of being rejected, and we wrestled until I saw myself, and it was only when I accepted and did not defend myself that He changed my name! I am no longer who man says I am, but who God says I am. My progress and my process will continue as God continues to expose the enemy that was living inside of me.

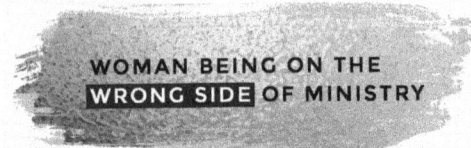

WOMAN BEING ON THE WRONG SIDE OF MINISTRY

Chapter 8
The Call
IS IT GODLY OR IS IT YOU?

Revelation 3:20

Behold, I stand at the door, and knock: if any man hear My Voice, and open the door, I will come in to Him, and will sup with Him, and he with Me.

From a noticeably early age, I have always felt different. Not that I thought I was better, but different. I spent a lot of alone time questioning my very existence. I would always question within myself: Why was I born with these unusual blue eyes? Why am I deaf in my right ear? Why do I have a speech impediment? Why was I always blamed for stuff that I did not do? These questions may not seem significant to the average person, but to me these were things that consumed my mentality every day.

As I stated in my earlier chapter "What Entered my Mind," the fear of the unknown has always given me anxiety. The thought of knowing that I was going to a sanctified church was opening the door of fear... and now I'm entering this little sanctified church and I'm seeing people jumping and shouting around a wood burning heater.

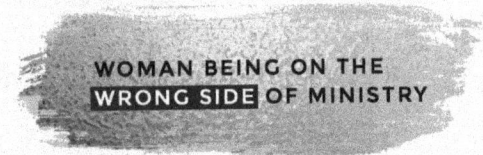

There was an older lady hitting two woodblocks together as if she were clapping her hands. There was a younger girl dancing around that heater with her eyes closed and her hands stretched out as if she was going to faint. You may be wondering why I am giving so much detail, well, let me explain. Not only was all of that happening, but there was something happening to me also, as I was captivated by that young girl that was about my age. To me, she looked so free and, for the first time, I found myself being drawn into that atmosphere as my hands began to clap to the beat of the bass drum and those wood blocks. It was as if the more I clapped, the faster my hands began to clap. It was as if something or someone invisible was clapping my hands for me.

The fear of the unknown was bringing on my anxiety, but then I felt myself being lifted up from where I was sitting and my feet were beginning to move all by themselves. I could no longer control what I was doing. There was a force stronger than I that was moving me around and about, but I felt so free and at peace. I could not control it or explain it.

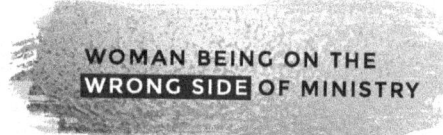

After some time, the drum slowed down and I was able to regain my composure. I felt weird and different at the same time and, looking at my siblings, I noticed that they were looking at me in awe, shocked to say the least. I looked to what was called the pulpit and there was the prophet staring out at the small gathering that was waiting to hear a Word from the Lord. You couldn't hear a pin drop. Back then, there was a great reverence for prophets sent by God.

My mom took us every night for the duration of that revival. She would bring gallon jugs of water for the prophet to pray over and bless. There was a special bottle just for me because of my hearing problem. I had to drink that blessed water every morning, one for the Father, Son, and Holy Spirit. I wanted to be healed so badly that I would just keep drinking past the Father, Son and Holy Spirit. My mother had her own health issues as well. She had developed asthma. I can still remember seeing my mother gasping for air during that time of the year when the pollen, ragweed and other plants were in full bloom.

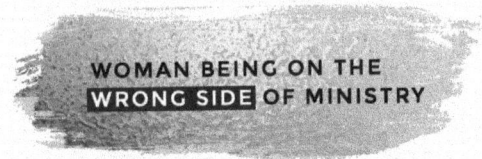

My mother's physician at that time recommended that she relocate to another state with less trees, pollen and other plants that were restricting her breathing.

Shortly afterward, we moved to New York City, Brooklyn to be exact. I thought to myself, now I'm free! hoping that my mother would never expose me to another sanctified church!

In the Book of Jeremiah 29:11, Jeremiah reminds us that God knows the plans that he has for us! My mother's health restricted her from working outside the home, so she started babysitting for a single parent, who had an aunt that worked at the postal service in Brooklyn. I will call her Ms. Prayer Warrior. She was such a sweet, kind and loving person, who had two beautiful daughters and was expecting another baby at that time.

Ms. Prayer Warrior took a liking to me. I would go home with her sometimes to watch her daughters. While she was preparing dinner, we would have play time. She was just like my second mother and I had gained two little sisters. I would often sleep over on
the weekends.

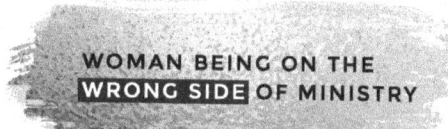

I learned quickly from my sleepovers that you just don't go to bed without praying, so I would recite the "Now I lay me down to sleep prayer", but Ms. Prayer Warrior would take her prayer up to a place where God was sitting on His throne. She would be weeping and crying and pleading with God for hours I would fall asleep at the foot of her bed, only to awake the next morning to the smell of breakfast cooking. We all were still at the foot of her bed where we had fallen asleep while she was praying. I was experiencing a prayer encounter at a very young age.

After living in New York for about five plus years, we relocated back to South Carolina. My mother never returned to that sanctified church and I was so relieved. Finally, I could live a different kind of life. In my high school years, I had a little more freedom and before long I was fascinated with dating boys. This trend continued throughout my high school years.

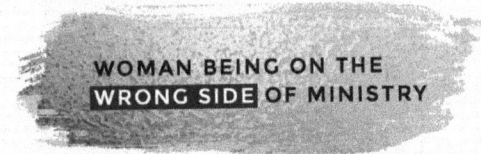

In chapter 2, I shared that I graduated high school in May of 1977 and I gave birth to my first son on June 10, 1977. Yes, a lot had taken place in my life in a short span of time. Soon after giving birth to my son, I married his father. I gave birth to another son two years later and, two years after that, I was divorced. Later that year, I met Jack from chapter 1, and we married in June of 1983. We had a son in January of the following year. Jack was deployed to Giessen, West Germany, and shortly afterward our children and I would join him overseas.

I can remember the first time I flew on an airplane, when I flew to El Paso, Texas. I heard so many horror stories about flying, those fables were beginning to cause me anxiety, but as the airline stewardess was walking the aisles to assure that our seats were in the upright position, she looked at me holding my toddler son and smiled. It was at that moment that my fear of flying began to subside.

That was just the beginning of my flying adventure. Since that time, you can call me a frequent flyer with SkyMiles.

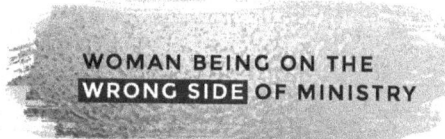

My longest flight was to Frankfurt, West Germany to reunite with Jack. I think that flight was about fourteen hours long, and what an experience it was, as I was traveling with a six month old baby that cried almost the entire flight, a five years old that was unhappy about flying to the point of throwing up, and a seven years old that seemed to be adjusting just fine. I was so relieved to arrive in Frankfurt and reunite with Jack. At that time, we were still very much newlyweds and we had so many dreams for our future and our family.

I struggled at first, adjusting to the time difference and with a young baby and two other children. I really needed to make our house a home. I eventually concluded that I needed a job to help with our family's needs. At that time, Jack was just an E-4 and we needed extra income. I am a helper and I am not allergic to work. I came from a legacy of hard workers. I wanted to help and not stress Jack, so I sought out employment. I was knowledgeable about cashiering, sewing, and retail, and I was a fast learner of any other trade jobs. My grandfather raised all of his grands to know a little bit about everything.

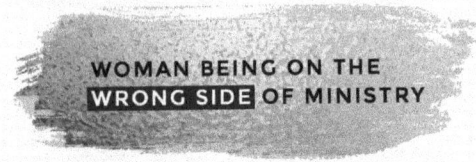

One evening after work I met a neighbor in our stairwell. We later became what I called stairwell friends, since that seemed to be our place of meeting. Sometimes we would talk for hours. She was a stay at home mom and I was a working mom. She was a devoted church goer as well and she finally asked me to visit her church. Going to church was the farthest thing from my mind. I wanted to go out and party, as my siblings would say. I left my mother's house at eighteen to be free from her rules and control, but I married someone that was worse than my mom. I divorced him five years later because he was extremely jealous and physically abusive, and now I'm free to finally find "Mr. Good Time."

I went out one weekend to a house party in the neighborhood and it was that night that changed my whole life. It was that night that I realized that there was no such thing as a "good time." After returning home, I sat on the bed, very disgusted with the course of events that had happened at that house party. As I was laying down, I heard a voice that I had never heard before saying, "Go to Church." I was so frightened by that voice that I could not sleep.

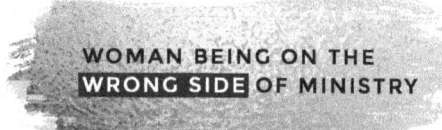

I was laying there having a conversation in my head with that voice. I was debating with what I know now was the Spirit of God. I said to the Spirit, "But I am not done having fun at the clubs yet!" For some reason, however, I knew it was the same Spirit that was drawing me when I was a young girl. It was drawing me again and I knew this time it was time for me to change.

That morning, I shared my experience with Jack and he agreed to go with me to church. I was so scared when I entered that church. I just knew that the entire building was going to collapse, but it didn't! That was the beginning of me rekindling my relationship with God! He won me over with His love. I fell in love with God and His Word…there was not enough time in a day for me to have Him. I just wanted more and more of him each and every day. I committed my life to Jesus, got water baptized. I felt brand new. Later, I received the baptism of the Holy Ghost with the evidence of speaking in other tongues. Yes, this girl was beginning to catch on fire!

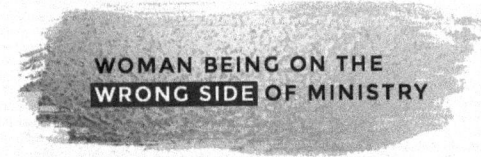

I became zealously sanctified just like those ladies at that little church in Hampton, South Carolina. I stopped wearing makeup and started wearing long dresses and bobby socks. Keeping my hair styled was not a priority. I was conforming to holiness in every way that I had seen others live it. It wasn't long before Jack began looking at other women. He had taken a night manager's job at one of the local night clubs. He worked mostly weekends, so I was always home with our children. There were a few times when he came home with watches that he said he found. Another time, he came home with a man's gold chain that he said he also found. There were phone calls where the person hung up when I answered. I know what you are thinking…my hindsight would suggest that I go out and get myself that blonde wig, but I loved Jack so much that I never suspected him of having an affair. One day, he just came home, looked me in the eyes and said, "Linda, I'm seeing another woman." My heart immediately started racing.

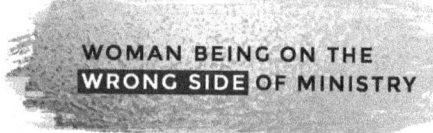

I was shocked at what Jack was saying, but being a godly wife, I forgave him immediately.

I began to seek godly advice from the older women at my church and, through much prayer and fasting and some wardrobe and makeup adjustments, I sought to rekindle our marriage. Let me be clear when I say that being in a strange country away from family really helped me to grow in my relationship with God and in my marriage. I became a better wife, mother and housekeeper. I learned a lot. I believed that my marriage had survived a great test as we were moving back to the United States. The military had assigned Jack to a base on the West Coast, and we were traveling there with some critical challenges, but we prayed and believed and God restored him.

We were forever grateful.

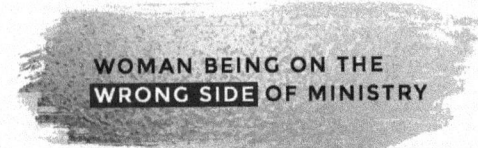

WOMAN BEING ON THE WRONG SIDE OF MINISTRY

Chapter 9
My Way or God's Word
NOT MY WILL

Proverbs 14:12

There is a way which seemeth right unto a man, but the end thereof are the ways of death.

After returning to the states, we immediately connected with a Gospel Service at our new duty station on the West Coast, Kino Gospel Service to be exact. We were told prior to leaving Germany that Kino was a very loving and nurturing church. We had no doubt and everyone at that church was very helpful in getting us settled.

When Jack signed into his new duty station, he carried a large gold envelope secured by tape. We had been praying that God would vindicate him of the accusation against him. I was a God-fearing prayer warrior that learned how to pray while overseas. My mentor of prayer, Mother Mary Stuart, would knock on my door every Tuesday for noonday prayer. At first, I used to hide from her and pretend that I was not home, but I was convicted. I am so glad that she never gave up on me... she was very persistent.

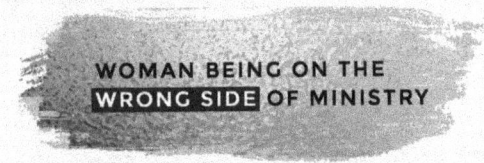

Those prayer meetings introduced me to the presence of God, where I learned how to hear His voice and to bear my soul to Him, to be intimate in fellowship with Him, and to be empowered by his Holy Spirit.

Jack was not going to do another tour in the military. His previous company Commander did not care for him at all, and to this day I still don't know the facts behind why she hated him so much. All I know is that whatever Jack told me, I believed him. The soldier handling incoming personnel at Jack's new duty station opened the sealed gold envelope and looked at my husband, then he looked at me. He then took the papers, tore them up and put them in the trash. I could not stop giving God praise. He covered Jack again! With that situation behind us, we were now able to focus on getting connected to our new house of worship under our new pastor.

We were connecting well at our new church. We met the Smith family, who were living in the same housing complex where we would soon be living and who would become a bridge in my life in years to come.

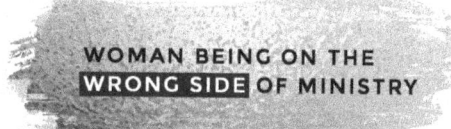

We met the Johnson family, whose wife Laura would become my friend for life. She has green eyes and mine, of course, are blue...we have a unique way of talking to each other (lol). I also met My Dearest Mother Julia McCaa, who has remained a strong anchor in my spiritual foundation. I'm forever grateful for her wisdom and encouragement, coupled with prayer. It was not long afterward that I accepted the call on my life. I was assigned a spiritual mentor to train me in the ministry as an aspiring missionary.

I had some great spiritual mentors at that church and I made some good friends as well. Our leadership was pleased to have us as part of their ministry. I had started working at the U.S. Army dining facility right across from Jack's company. Since all of our children were of school age, we were free from the stress of hiring a babysitter. We were faithful to our church and it was not long afterward that Jack accepted his call in the ministry and was licensed as a minister of the gospel service. I was so happy for him. The late Dr. Clea McCaa Sr. took him under his guidance and tutorial, mentoring him to pray, study and serve the people of God.

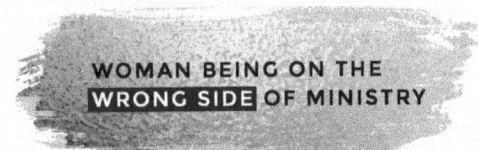

Shortly afterwards, I acknowledged my calling into the gospel ministry. One dear brother in the Lord at that time had shared a profound Word from the Lord with me that I can still hear as clear as the exact day he spoke it. My brother said to me that, God really wants to use my mouth, but as much as God wants to use my mouth…the devil wants to use it too. I still struggle with my mouth daily, but I was progressing every day to assure this calling is Godly and not of me, being connected with a local ministry at the base was my direct accountability, Jack, however, wanted to leave to support another ministry, so I followed him. It was hard for me to leave Kino, but I wanted to support Jack. Then he left that ministry and I followed him again and it was at that particular ministry that I began to see him being used. Some years later, he was forced to retire after having served fifteen years active duty in the U.S. Army. Shortly afterward, my friend Eugene would find me working at my salon. I was so surprised to see him. In his excitement, the first words out of his mouth after we exchanged greetings was, "Linda, I can't believe you and Jack haven't started your own ministry yet."

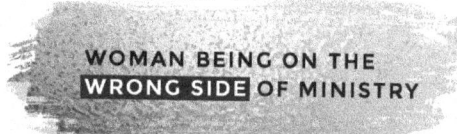

WOMAN BEING ON THE WRONG SIDE OF MINISTRY

I just froze right there. I didn't have an answer, but I had a confirmation as to what I felt the Lord was leading us to. That evening, I would share with Jack what our friend Eugene had said to me. Jack looked as if he was relieved to hear it as well, and it was not long afterward that Jack accepted his call to pastorship.

Chapter 10
Being on The Wrong Side of Ministry

WORKING FOR THE WRONG MASTER

1 Corinthians 7:33-34

But he that is married careth for the things that are of the world, how he may please his wife. **34** There is difference also between a wife and a virgin. The unmarried woman careth for the things of the Lord, that she may be holy both in body and in spirit: but she that is married careth for the things of the world, how she may please her husband.

Living out west was the most challenging time of my walk with God. I was pursuing God's presence and His divine revelation through prayer and fasting. I was a dedicated believer, wife, mother, and entrepreneur of my own hair salon. I still had time to have dinner once a week with my husband (our me time), family time with the kids, church prayer, Bible study and choir rehearsal and still worked a full-time job. When Jack shared with me his calling to pastorship, we both began to seek God through prayers for direction. We knew that whom God calls, he would establish. There were quite a few churches in the local community and we knew that our assignment was to go out of the city, but little did we know that God would send me back to my hometown to start our ministry.

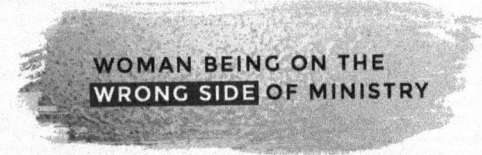

WOMAN BEING ON THE WRONG SIDE OF MINISTRY

We were both excited when we got the confirmation through prayer and our spiritual fathers that we looked up to, our destination was confirmed! We started purchasing items for our new church. Many that believed in our vision sowed financial seeds into our ministry as well. We were so excited to serve the people of God and I, for one, felt very secure in my marriage. After all that we had experienced in Germany, we both had matured in the ways of God to the point that we would talk about it and then pray about it and believe in God for the healing of or deliverance from whatever we were facing in our marriage. I felt that we were doing just fine.

We founded our ministry in October of 1997 in Hampton, South Carolina in the study of the home we were renting. We started having weekly Bible study and the ministry eventually grew out of our home and into a rented building. After painting, carpeting and decorating, the sanctuary in which we prayed was hallowed to God. We saw souls saved and delivered, receiving the baptism of the Holy Spirit.

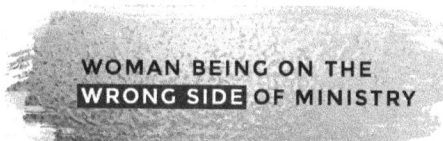

We had a praise and worship team and a choir that would sing under the anointing of God. We hosted prayer meetings and revivals, friends and family day picnics, women and men conferences. We were really making a difference in our small community, or so I thought, but old traditions of the south and my past mistakes would begin to resurface and cause me to feel very indifferent to certain family members and to people in general. Jack would tell me things that other females were saying to him about me that would cause me to doubt my very purpose. The sad thing about all of it was that he never ever said that he had defended me.

It was then that I started to speak out as if I had to defend myself from all of this traditional practice. I had developed such a strong bond with most of the women at our church. We would have women's meetings and share with each other and to this day, I love them all for what they sowed into my life. Even though they would say that I blessed them, I would say that we equally blessed each other. The Lord blessed us to minister for over six years before we would move back to the West Coast. We returned with our sons and six other families seeking a change and a new beginning in their lives.

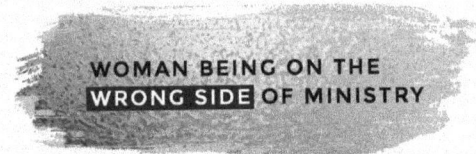

We birthed our ministry in the local community. We settled into our home and assisted the other families in finding housing and jobs. We were moving and seeking God by faith for all that we needed. God began to show his seal of approval on the ministry as souls began to come out and accept the Lord as their personal Savior, joining the church and beginning to grow in ministry.

I served as the church administrator because I knew the vision of the house. I wanted to free Jack from having to worry about certain administrative needs. I loved him. He was not just my husband, but my man of God, and it was a joy to serve him and to help him further the ministry. We went through several name changes during our ministry, as well as building expansions, new leases and finally our church building. I did everything I could to support Jack while also working. This new building project was becoming very challenging and frustrating at times. I'm not very patient with people who give excuses instead of solutions, especially when they are wearing the title of leader.

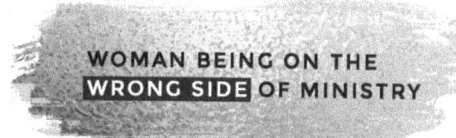

Administration was my strength and Jack's weakness, so he gave me the responsibility of handling all of the administrative needs, which made me look bossy or controlling to mostly the men in the ministry. And again, to this day, I do not think he ever defended my actions to any of them. I know that I have a strong personality and I am proud of the woman that God has made me to be. I am not perfect, but I am still God's favorite. I have worked tirelessly for countless hours preparing programs, booklets, new member classes, prayer journals, plays, Christmas parties, and event decorating. You name it, I did it and I did it all for God first and Jack, always showing him how much I cared for him and confirming that I loved him.

When we, as the body of Christ, agreed to move our ministry into our own stand-alone building, we were excited. I found a vacant office building in town. Sticking with the vision that we were called to, I assisted in the planning of the church and the demolishing of part of the building. All of the members assisted in removing debris and in painting, cleaning and setting up our newly renovated sanctuary.

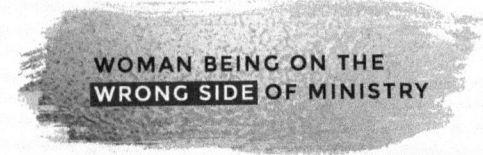

WOMAN BEING ON THE WRONG SIDE OF MINISTRY

Needless to say, we were excited. The following month, we dedicated our church to the Lord. We ordained Elders and appointed Deacons and Deaconesses. We spent the rest of that year fine tuning the ministry, holding committee meetings with our board, of which I served as the 2nd Vice President, and continuing to share in the planning of further endeavors. Little did I know that my life was about to shift.

It was late September and it was just beginning to cool off a little from a very hot summer. I was back driving a school bus and working from my salon at home as well as attending church meetings and Bible studies, and I still found time to counsel when needed. I would prepare dinner on my morning school break to make sure that it would be ready that evening. Jack was bouncing around between jobs. I tried to support him as much as I could while he searched for suitable work. In October of 2016, he became very annoyed and frustrated with a few members at the church, or some pastors in the community, with which he could not seem to connect.

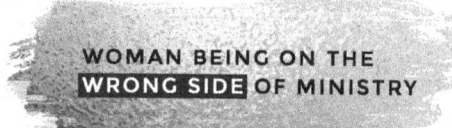

He began to say to me and to the members of our congregation that in 2017, he was going to remove some people from his life. I immediately asked him who and why? He never gave me an answer or any indication that I was one of the people that he would be removing.

I kept on doing everything I normally did for our home and church as well as anything else that he needed. I was beginning to suffer greatly from menopause and I was experiencing severe anxiety and mood swings. I sought help from my doctor and she wanted me to take hormone replacement medication. I refused it and began to look into all-natural medication instead. I shared my emotional, moody attitude with Jack and, to me, he seemed concerned. He even sent me some research on menopause. We were researching this together, and I was so touched that he showed concern for my situation. Later that month, I went back to my doctor and shared with her again that I needed some help with my menopause symptoms. She ran a hormone test and gave me a prescription for an all-natural hormone cream.

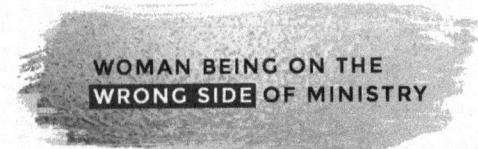

I was forever grateful. I started using it, but it would take about a month for it to get into my system before I noticed any change in my attitude and mood swings. Later, I was beginning to feel like a woman again.

In January of 2016, Jack was fired from his state job. I was devastated, but remained very calm and very understanding as he shared with me that he did not know why he had been fired. He told me they just told him that he was to pack up and leave. I still remember walking my client out to her car after her hair appointment and seeing all of the pictures I had brought to decorate his office packed in the backseat of the car. At that point, my heart began to race as I was experiencing anxiety, fearing the unknown.

In April of 2016, Jack took a job as a health technician at a local facility, where he enjoyed his work. I may have stopped by once or twice, but because of the HIPAA law, I never wanted to put him in an awkward position.

He worked where lots of sensitive paperwork needed to be entered into the data portal daily that dealt with patient privacy and sometimes kept him out later than normal work hours. As a wife, I understood. The workload was becoming increasingly longer with late client meetings. We were both working very hard to keep our bills paid, due to Jack's bouncing around from job to job with less and less pay. Plus, anyone that knows Jack knows that he has a large appetite for stuff. He has to have the biggest and the best of everything. His desires and my love for him kept me always working to make sure we could cover all of our expenses. I had about 12 plus credit cards that I had used for trips, stuff for both of our parents, clothes, electronics and anything else that he wanted.

Jack was also a very flashy dresser with a lot of charm. For thirty-four plus years, he was charming me, until he had exhausted everything I had: my mind, body, soul, credit cards and bank account. I was so stressed out with debt and going through menopause did not help with all my mood swings.

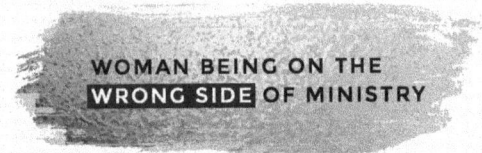

To add to that, the church membership was not growing and he blamed me. Everything was always my fault. He was gifted, with "it was not I" anointing. He was always perfect, never did any wrong, had an answer for everything and everyone. You see, that is why I loved him for all those years, but in the months to come, I would be in for the shock of my life!

In December of 2016, we did not have our yearly Christmas party for the members of the church. Things were beginning to be a little different. I had my own issues with my body and I knew that Jack was still working long hours and was extremely tired, to the point of eating dinner and falling asleep in the recliner. I was planning our annual Black History Program, spending long hours researching and writing the script. I am a very visual person, so when God began to give me visions, I internalized them and I was focused! The program that year was a big success and I was convinced that that was my last one. The people were so blessed by that program and the accolades just kept coming to the point of tears.

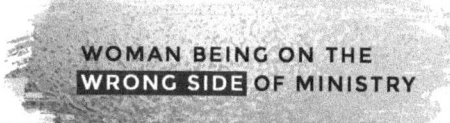

I was overwhelmed.

I told Jack earlier, during rehearsals, that I would not do the Black History Program the following year. I exited the building in order to gain my composure when Jack came out and said that I had to do it again because the people loved it. That meant so much to me, seeing that he was pleased.

In February of 2017, Jack's birthday was coming up and, because of the Christmas holidays, we had exhausted most of our credit cards, but I wanted to get him something special. Anyone that knows Jack knows that he likes expensive stuff. January was pastor's appreciation month, and he had asked the church to give me a pastor's appreciation instead of him. I was so honored that he didn't want to be appreciated, but I'm a wife first and my home comes first and whatever was sown into me was sown into us, that was how we lived and that was the level of trust that we had in our marriage. I used the funds to pay off Jack's credit cards first, because they were less than mine. Our goal was to pay them all off and cut them up, only keeping two for emergencies.

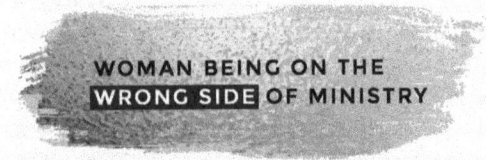

One weekend after the appreciation, while I was working on a church program, I went to make a cup of tea and realized that I needed some honey. I asked Jack if he would go to the store for me and he said sure and asked what I needed. I said that I just needed some honey for my tea. He took out his phone and typed in honey, then asked if I needed anything else, and I said no. He left saying that he would be right back. Over one hour later, he arrived with a container of coffee but no honey. I was working in our office the entire time waiting on him to bring me the honey, so I said, "Babe, this is not honey." He looked at me and said, "Oh, I'm sorry, babe. I thought you said coffee." I said, "Why you... **(I had a few choice words for Mr.)**, Jack was so upset with me, what I said was so convenient now that I'm looking back. I did immediately apologize for my poor choice of words, and asked for his forgiveness. He wouldn't speak to me much after that, but we still talked about other things. We watched TV shows, ate dinner, went to church, checked on each other during the day, etc.

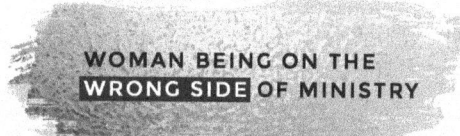

I was able to get Jack the PlayStation VR for his birthday. He was so happy, I was glad that I was able to purchase it with my credit cards, even though they were almost maxed out. I knew that the game would put a smile on his face. On his actual birthday every year, I would make him a Facebook page, so that family and friends could comment on it. As I looked at some of the comments, I noticed that he was commenting on everyone's comment but mine, so I gave him a call to ask him if he liked the post. He said yes, so I asked why he was commenting on everyone's post but mine. He said that he wanted to thank me personally and I asked him, why? If you are thanking everyone else, you can thank me, too. He said that it's hard to thank someone that calls you (a few choice words), I told him that I apologized and asked him to forgive me and he said that he would talk to me when he got home. When he came home, I waited and he said nothing. I asked if we were going to talk and he said, "Not today, I'm tired. We will talk tomorrow."

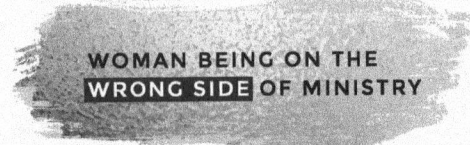

WOMAN BEING ON THE WRONG SIDE OF MINISTRY

The next day, he went to work and when he came home for lunch, I asked him yet again when we were going to talk. He looked at me and said, "Linda, I love you but **I want a divorce.**" Then, he began listing stuff that he said I did to him over the years. He kept on babbling, and all I could hear myself saying was, **"Wow, I'm on the wrong side of ministry."** As he vented, I was just looking at him. I didn't know who he was and I felt so bad inside that this man could not see anything I had done or sacrificed for our family, marriage or ministry. To him, I was the worst person on the face of the Earth. **When I was able to get a word in, I asked just one question, "Who is she?"** His reply was that there was no one. I said ok, but just know that I am not giving you a divorce. He stood there and yelled, "I am afraid of you Linda and I will not live the latter part of my life like I did the first part." I then asked him again, "Who is she?", because someone had been speaking in his ears. I spent that afternoon searching inside myself to see where I had failed him.

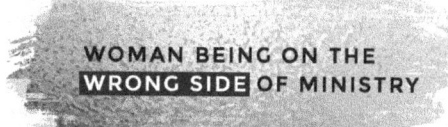

WOMAN BEING ON THE WRONG SIDE OF MINISTRY

How long had he felt this way about me? How did I wind up on the wrong side of ministry with a man that would get up in the pulpit and express his love for me one day and then hate my guts the next day, I really needed God to help me process what was happening to me and to my marriage.

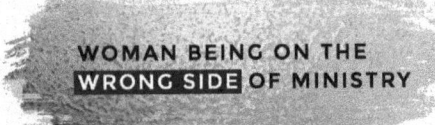

Chapter 11

Where Did It Fall Off At?

WAS BLIND, BUT NOW I SEE

2 Kings 4-7

So he went with them. And when they came to Jordan, they cut down wood. **5** But as one was felling a beam, the axe head fell into the water: and he cried, and said, Alas, master! for it was borrowed. **6** And the man of God said, Where fell it? And he shewed him the place. And he cut down a stick and cast it in thither; and the iron did swim. **7** Therefore said he, Take it up to thee. And he put out his hand and took it.

The Axe

To this day I can still play out that day, February 11, 2017, when all hell was unleashed on my marriage. It was a losing battle ever since he spoke it out of his mouth, as if he had premeditated everything. I didn't have a clue as to what was happening to us. I eventually went on an absolute fast. It was easy for me because my anxiety, stress, and fear of the unknown were spinning out of control. Jack had many faces, so I never knew who was coming home or who I would be talking to. I was very naive to worldly tactics and I still wanted to trust him at his word as a wife should. After all, he was a pastor and the priest of our home.

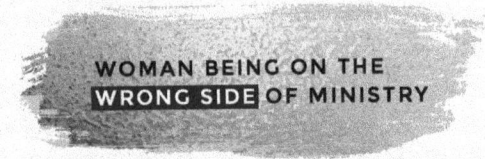

I was devastated to know that I had hurt him to the point that he wanted to end our marriage. I began to seek wise counsel from my mentors and spiritual mother. I was crushed to the core of my heart every time I replayed in my mind Jack saying that he was afraid of me. I could not get those words out of my mind. I kept thinking that we didn't fight; that we may have disagreements, but what couple did not? I knew our marriage was not perfect, but it was not that bad either. Something had happened, and I was being set up.

It was not long afterward, that same week to be exact, that I was home and happened to see Jack's iPad by his bedside, so I picked it up and I logged on, since I knew his password. We had complete trust in sharing our phones, iPads and computers. His messenger page was open, so I read some of his text messages, and I was overwhelmed by the language that Jack used with a female co-worker. My heart began to race as I was reading his text messages and her replies.

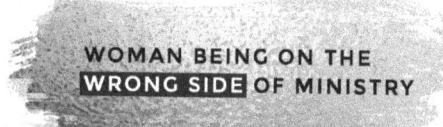

I took pictures of all of their text messages, then I called and confronted him. He immediately came home and got his iPad to delete the texts, like I was stupid enough not to copy them, and the lady...I was so disappointed. She was someone that I knew and respected. But the bravest thing to do in a situation like this is to forgive quickly. He asked me to forgive him and I did. He also started looking for another job.

From that point on, the trust was gone. I tried to stay focused because of the church and not let my emotions get the best of me. I found a local therapist and started counseling once a week. I bared my soul to this therapist. Jack came twice, just to see if I was being helped. He seemed concerned and I really wanted him to be. He never came to another session, but I continued to see that therapist once a week.

One afternoon, I was shopping at the store right by Jack's workplace and, as I went to start the truck, it would not start.

I phoned Jack and he said to come get the car, that he would get the truck when he got off. I don't know if he told her to leave before I got there, but as I was turning the corner, she was leaving the building, walking in my direction. I began to pray immediately, asking God to word my mouth because I was going to address her about her disgusting text messages.

She was walking past me when I asked her if I could I talk with her for a minute. She stopped and the look on her face was of fear that I was going to whip her tail or make a loud scene, but, being the woman of God that I am and feeling that she was very lonely and vulnerable and just wanted someone to pay attention to her, I just wanted to speak to her about her integrity. She was someone that I admired and looked up to. I had met her through a mutual friend when she worked at the local hospital. I was always there for the birth of the members of our congregation and she was always kind to me. I had no intention of doing any bodily harm to her, and to Jack's alluring charm, I will say this.... My vows were with Jack and not with her, however it showed me that hurt women often hurt one another.

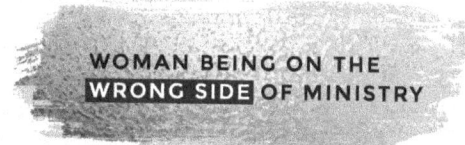

I was told that an extramarital affair destroyed her marriage, which had also ended in divorce, and now she would play a part in destroying mine.

I told her that I forgave her and that I would pray that the Lord would send her a man that was not someone else's husband. By that time, Jack was coming out of the building to see what I was saying to her. I told him that I handled it, got the keys and left. Driving home, I thanked God for giving me the words to let her know that I forgave her. In the weeks to come, I would continue to go faithfully to therapy every week. That was my release and my healing. Believe me when I tell you that, if I had not chosen to be the problem, I never would have found my healing. Jack went to counseling twice, as I stated earlier, but that was it. I knew that he was checking out of our marriage, but what I didn't know was that in the months to come, he would make the most treacherous accusation against me, unleashing the most demonic attack against my character, trying to expose me as a husband abuser.

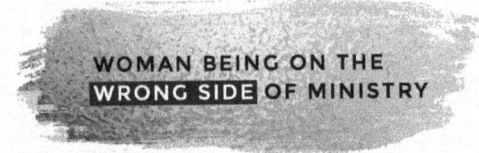

In May of 2017, Jack went to the East Coast for Mother's Day, to visit his mom at the church's expense. We were having problems and the church thought that we both should take some time off. I was to accompany him, but he didn't think that was a good idea. He said that us being apart would make our hearts grow fonder. In other words, he didn't want me to go. The church board then agreed to send us both to a spirit-led counselor to help us work through this difficult time. While Jack was away, it was hard to reach him on his cellphone, but he would call me at very odd times. For days I called, only to get no answer. One time I called Jack about our dog and he went off on me, as if he was showing off to someone that he handles me. I quickly apologized and I would not call him again.

At the end of the school year in May 2017, as I stated in Chapter 7, I went to Hawaii to visit my mentor Toni, to get some rest and spiritual refreshing. I was truly blessed to be away from my small city and to be at the beach in Hawaii.

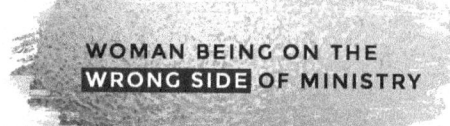

There is something cleansing about that water that caused me to release all of my stress, tension, anxiety and fears. It was as if every wave that came in took bits and pieces of my concern away. I felt alive again and I had renewed strength and confidence to believe God regarding my marriage and to trust Him to heal all of my trust issues concerning Jack. I returned home renewed and refreshed. Jack picked me up from the airport. I had a late flight, so we spent the night out of town. That morning, we drove back home. We made small talk and listened to music. He really liked listening to oldies and he knew all the words to the songs playing on the station. I knew some of the words, but not all of them. I just went along with whatever he wanted to keep the peace.

When I arrived home, there was a very odd smell in the house, like someone had burned incense. I asked what that smell was and he replied that it was air freshener because he had forgotten to take the trash out. I said OK, but my intuition was telling me differently.

When he left for work, I got my anointed oil, put it in a spray bottle, and went through every room in the house praying and speaking in tongues; casting that foul spirit out of my house. I believe that Jack had a female in our home while I was in Hawaii. I immediately got my prayer CD for marriages and I let it play 24/7. I was in warfare for my marriage and I was not going to let the devil destroy what God had joined together.

June was a special month for me, as I would be celebrating another birthday. Jack worked late the day of my birthday. He said that he had to input his data in the computer, and I said OK. Jack came home around 11:30 PM. I waited up for him and he looked at me and said, "Oh, Happy Birthday. I'm sorry I didn't have any money to buy you anything." I said it was OK, but deep inside, I was mad as hell. I sensed that he was lying, as usual, and he smelled funny, so I knew he was not at work, but I believed in the power of prayer. I knew through the Word of God that my place was to be at home, regardless of what I thought I knew. As long as he was coming home, there was still hope.

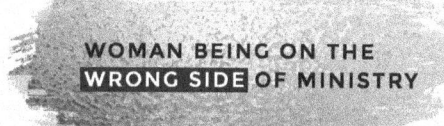

Jack and I have always shared joint banking accounts with direct deposit. Most of our bills were automatic debit to assure that they were paid on time. It was in July of 2017 that I noticed that there was no direct deposit from Jack's paycheck. I brought it to Jack's attention. It was then that I found out that he had changed banks and that I had no access to the new account, but he assured me that he would manually pay the outstanding bills that were piling up in our joint account with overdrafts. I tried to remain calm and trust him to do the right thing, as I am one that believes in paying bills and Jack is very materialistic. I confessed earlier that I have a few issues and one is a fear of not paying bills on time. I have always handled the bill paying for our home and I was relieved and scared at the same time when I was not in control of when our bills were being paid, but I had to pray and trust that Jack was on top of our bills, and so I trusted God with it.

On July 20, 2017, Jack and I had breakfast and Jack left for work. I went into my salon. I had a braid client scheduled and the service took about four hours.

Afterward, I called Jack to check in.

He told me that he was at work. I had to run some errands in town, so I was going to Jack's job to switch vehicles, but he kept insisting that I drive the truck, even though I really wanted to drive the car. We went back and forth a few times and finally I asked where he was. He replied that he was out of town getting the tires rotated. I asked why he didn't tell me, as I would have loved to go with him to get out of our little town for a minute. He replied that he needed some time to think, so I said that I would see him later. I waited all evening for Jack to come home. I knew we had friends in that town that were also pastors and I just assumed he was spending time with them.

I waited up for hours and was starting to worry that something had happened to him. I called his phone throughout that day and night. I was in our bedroom, sitting on our bed looking at his dresser, the corner where he had his clothes, when I realized that he had taken one of the suitcases. I was sitting there thinking to myself: I have been working two jobs, getting up at five o'clock every morning Monday through Friday, leaving Jack in bed sleeping (or so I thought).

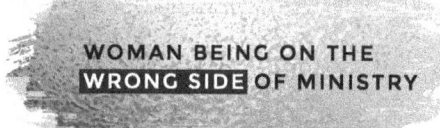

Jack's past had let me know that he was once again being dishonest with me. I was disappointed, but not mad. I know that God was carrying me through this discovery of what had probably been going on for some time. I can say this now that I'm divorced from Jack: he had always craved more and more attention, as if I was never enough.

I had always worked as a child, and my work ethic was enhanced in my adulthood to help support my family. While working long hours in the hair salon and on weekends, then at church on Sundays, I was just too busy for my own good and too exhausted and spiritually weak to even notice that he was not just deceiving me. The entire church was being rocked to sleep by his deceptive spirit. I eventually called the police to file a missing person report. He finally called after I spoke with our youngest son and shared with him that I had filed a missing person report. He said that he was OK and that he was heading out to clear his head and to think.

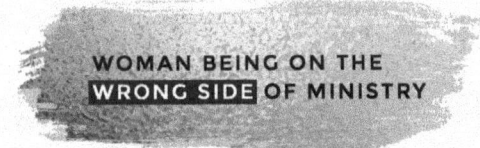

I did not see Jack again until that next week, Tuesday at about 7:30 am. When he walked in, I was in our bedroom sitting on the bed. He looked at me and said good morning. I said good morning and he walked out of the room. I was sitting there thinking that he had some nerve walking in here after leaving me with barely any money and a truck that was a "may start and may go," abandoning the church that Sunday, leaving me to make excuses for his absence. I wanted to bust him down to his white meat, but instead of giving in to my flesh, I chuckled within myself. I must confess that I really wanted to kick his tail, and that's saying it with grace, but Clara Lee would have said it just the way she felt it. I kept thinking to myself girl...you have a fingerprint clearance card and you can't afford to lose your job! Thank God for ministering angels that kept speaking to my heart that day. I eventually asked him if we were good and if there was anything we needed to talk about, but he said that we were good.

That Wednesday afternoon, he decided to bring his suitcases in from his trip and sort through his clothes for laundry.

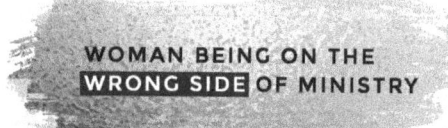

He showed me some shoes he said that he had bought, but they didn't look like shoes a pastor would wear. The colors were very bold: black patent leather with silver metallic and navy blue with a white floral pattern. They were definitely too flashy for me. He had lost his anointing and was backsliding into a worldly appetite. I respected the wedding vows that I had made to Jack, but I knew that we were in a different place concerning our marriage and I was praying to God for restoration. I still functioned as his wife, even after the abandonment. Jack went to work and I was sorting his laundry. Jack normally does the laundry, but this day I was home and my mind was racing concerning where Jack was for the last five days, so I decided to start the laundry. To my amazement, a receipt fell out of Jack's suit pocket, so I looked at it and it was for two movie tickets and dinner reservations. I then went out to our car to find a cooler with food that he doesn't even eat. Yes, I'm mad as hell now so I called him on it. He said that he was coming home to talk with me because he was with a client and hung up. Oh, hell no!!!, I now knew that the enemy was using him to provoke me...I needed to calm down and think!

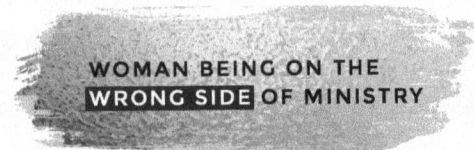

WOMAN BEING ON THE WRONG SIDE OF MINISTRY

I waited awhile but he didn't call, so I was going to stop by his job before going to the store, but I spotted our truck at the park. Thinking he was with his client, I decided to wait for him. I was parked right next to our truck when I saw him walking with a tall, fair-skinned female with reddish hair whom I didn't recognize. As I started walking toward him, he started running toward me, asking me where I was going. I looked at him and said, "How could you?" Jack kept pushing me back and I kept telling him to move out of my way. When I started walking toward the lady, she started avoiding me and then ran back into the park. I was mad as hell. Jack was holding me back, so his side chick could run away. I was crushed beyond measure and the thought of him restraining me while she ran away was the worst, at that point it was over for me. Jack got in the truck and left. I got in the car and I left too. We both went home.
I needed answers but he kept talking that New York City slang to me, and I lost it. I can't say what really happened, but I would have demolished that man if he had not left that house and yes, you thought right that he went straight to the police. Yes, my flesh was in full bloom and I was angry as hell.

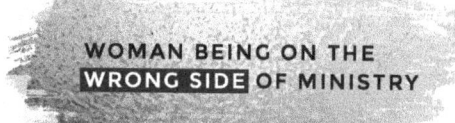

WOMAN BEING ON THE WRONG SIDE OF MINISTRY

Jack pressed assault charges against me, tried to charge me with check fraud, barred me from the church that I helped birth, took me off of the church bank accounts that I had established, voted me off the church board that I had put together, had my cell phone cut off, and deprived me of financial support for six months. He took me to family court to get a restraining order against me in order to have me thrown out of the house that we had built from the ground up. He told my sons that he was afraid of me, and I know he should have been after I caught him with another woman. I had marriage vows with him, not her, and I don't fight women over NO man. No amount of prayer or counseling was going to prevent me from taking my pain and anger out on him for destroying my trust, breaking my heart, and lying to me straight to my face. Oh yes, he needed to be gone.

While awaiting our court date, he convinced our sons to assist him in moving into our youngest son's house. Although I knew it was best for him to leave, I was not prepared to live alone. I hit rock bottom and at times I felt like just giving up.

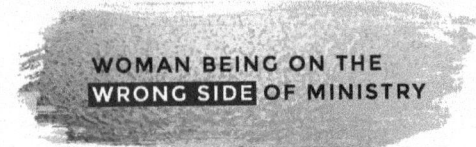

I fell into a depression and I felt like just ending it. At times, I was kicking and screaming to God until I had no more voice or tears. I was angry with God and I was having a meltdown. I couldn't understand why God was allowing the enemy to destroy my marriage. One night I woke up crying. I cried so much, and I screamed out to God, asking WHY? WHY? WHY? I found myself balled up in a fetal position just like a baby. I was just numb all over; no amount of wine was able to fill that void of pain that was in my heart. I remember video calling my friend Carla at about 2:00 am because my anxiety was out of control. I cried until my nose was clogged, my eyes were swollen and my voice hoarse. I felt like I was losing my mind and my friend Carla said something that made all the sense in this world. She said, "Linda, you are grieving the death of your marriage," and, for the first time since the breakup, it made perfect sense. My marriage was dead and I needed closure. The only way for me to get closure was to accept it and move on.

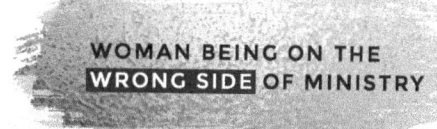

If it had not been for all the prayers and support of the churches in my community and the prayers of my family and friends near and far, I don't know how I could have made it out alive. In the days to come, I began to make peace with God. God then asked me a question, because he knew I was still hoping against hope with regard to my marriage and God wanted me to be sure that I was finished! God said to me, if I send Jack back and he apologizes to you and asks for forgiveness, will you take him back? I pondered it, knowing that I must forgive him, but to take him back with his lying, cheating, whoremongering self...I SAID HELL NO, and I WANT A DIVORCE, because I'm getting too old to play with immature spirits.

In the weeks to come, I learned that Jack had set me up to fail and I didn't have a clue. He convinced our sons to believe that I wasn't a good mother, that I treated them badly just like I treated him. My sons are my life, everything I did for them I meant for their own good. Even though I was not perfect, I still cared and there has never been a time when they needed me and I didn't show up.

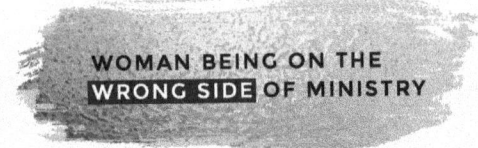

I have asked my children to forgive me if I had mistreated them in any way and for them to make all the necessary adjustments to be a better parent to their own children.

Within six months, I was suffering from the loss of my marriage. I was abandoned, my blood pressure skyrocketed and I was prescribed antidepressants. I had to learn to live by myself. I had to ask people to feed me, to put gas in my car. I stood in lines for food and assistance with my bills, all while still legally married to Jack. I eventually filed for divorce. The judge awarded me spousal maintenance support as long as I remain unmarried. Jack then wanted to reconcile with me, but I knew he was just trying not to pay me what the judge had awarded me. Jack may be a New York City slicker, but that judge despised him for how he had treated me after thirty-four years of marriage. Jack just kept putting his own foot in his mouth. I even felt sorry for him at times. The devil was really having his way with Jack.

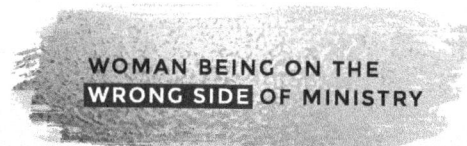

WOMAN BEING ON THE WRONG SIDE OF MINISTRY

The judge told him that what he did was called abandonment and then asked him how he preached to his congregation. The Judge then asked Jack what he thought was a fair settlement and Jack said two hundred and fifty dollars a month. The judge said that that was blatant disrespect after I had given thirty-four years of my life. I still do not know how I got there with Jack. One day he was telling the church how much he loved me and the next day he was telling me to my face that he hated me.

Being with Jack for 34 years of marriage and 24 plus years of ministry, no one could have convinced me that Jack would have done all of these horrific things to me…not in a million years. My true friends and family were in shock, just as I was. I witnessed members of our ministry crying because they too felt betrayed and used. There was no empathy from Jack at all. We were all very devastated.

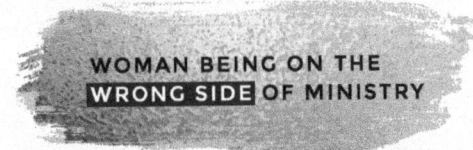

In the days and months to come, I embarked on finalizing this chapter of my journey as the Pastor's Wife, 1st Lady, Co-Pastor, and Spiritual Mother to an amazing congregation of believers. They will always be my Spiritual sons and daughters of the Faith, and they will also grow through this experience, just as I did. On January 24, 2018, I, Linda Yvette Foster, legally divorced Jack after thirty-four plus years. After the divorce papers were signed, stamped, and filed in court, I approached him, looked him in the eye, and thanked him for thirty-four years of marriage. In the following weeks, I packed up and prepared to leave the West Coast for a place I call recovery, but before that happened, I was given a beautiful going away by the most awesome group of Churches in that Community, who came together to give words of encouragement and prayers. I was so blessed by everyone and I will never forget them. Jack had told me for years that nobody in that city liked me and I believed him, but on that day, there were pastors, first ladies, church mothers, elders, ministers, and many sisters and brothers of the faith there that I love dearly.

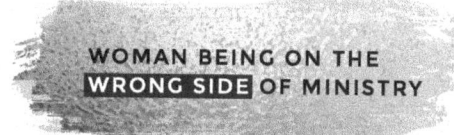

WOMAN BEING ON THE WRONG SIDE OF MINISTRY

Mother Julia McCaa gave words of encouragement, all the pastors present laid hands and prayed for my safe departure. I was so blessed that day. God made the devil a liar that day. I must say that my soul was rejoicing to see all the love shown to me. Thank you all for your Love. In the days to come, I had my moving truck loaded and my good friends the McGowans provided me with a room at their home until my departure. We have always remained friends despite the painful things that had happened to them while attending our church. Carl and Susie have always been loving, God-fearing people who ministered in a Spirit of hospitality. At their home, you are treated like family.

The morning of January 30, 2018, my truck was packed. My two favorite Deacons, whom I call Mike (Alonzo Sweet) and Ike (Roger Hunter), along with Elder Carl McGowan, were putting my car on the car carrier and tying it down, double checking that it was locked and secured. As I was saying my thank yous and goodbyes, Elder McGowan asked all that were present to join hands as he prayed for my safe departure.

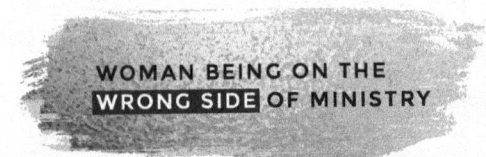

He asked God to release my Spirit from that city. At that moment, I was broken in my Spirit, my body was bowed in reverence to the Spirit of God that was present in that room… it was as if I was being birthed into a new beginning. I must admit it was hard but it was necessary that I was released from that area to go to my new assignment called recovery. I thank God for using Elder McGowan to pray that prayer of release. I said my goodbyes and picked up my spiritual daughter and co-worker Anitra, who would help me drive on my journey to the East Coast.

Leaving that city after about fifteen years was hard. As we passed through the small city, I was reflecting on the friends and memories that I had made there.
I personally had not chosen to leave, but I needed to rebuild my life as a single, saved, sanctified and broken woman of God. As we entered Interstate 10 heading east, Anitra drove first. She loves driving and it was an adventure trip for her. I was in charge of taking pictures of every state sign as we entered new states. Anitra was merging onto 10 East and there was an 18-wheeler in the right-hand lane also entering the freeway.

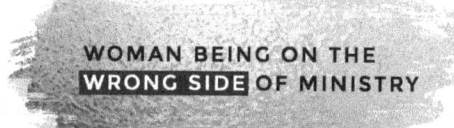

WOMAN BEING ON THE WRONG SIDE OF MINISTRY

Our trucks were parallel as we were driving into traffic. The 18-wheeler was merging close to the white line, and the force of that truck was drawing our truck towards it. Anitra was fighting to keep our truck from crashing into the 18-wheeler. I'm staring at the truck and watching Anitra fighting to keep us from crashing, and at that point I was full of anxiety and fear. The enemy was trying to stop me and even kill me! The deceptive plot of the enemy had failed.

God had released me from that state and the enemy was upset, but I was moving forward.

That day we made it to El Paso, Texas, got a room and had dinner. We would continue my journey in the morning. We were up fairly early and the weather was very nice. After fueling up and eating breakfast, we were back on the road. Anitra took the first drive out of El Paso. She is such a good driver and a good-hearted person. She didn't think twice about accompanying me on my journey. She wanted to do it and I am forever grateful. We made several stops for fuel, food and just to rest and stretch our bodies. Anitra was about 181 miles outside of Dallas, Texas when I took over the driving.

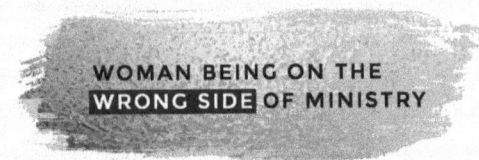

I was still dealing with a little fear and anxiety, but I was determined not to give in to the wiles of the devil, so I put in my ear plugs, turned on my worship music and went into the Holy of Holies and worshipped God, praying and singing in the spirit and rebuking the devil and decreeing victory. The more I prayed, the more I had peace. This was the first time I had ever driven a moving truck... and towing a car, too. For those of you who know me, you know that God was really stretching me out of my comfort zone, that was why I was praying so much and so hard...I was in Constant Warfare! I made it into Dallas about 6:00 – 6:30 pm.

I was feeling pretty good driving that big truck with my car in tow. I am a school bus driver by trade and I'm very comfortable driving a school bus, but this is a truck and trailer and I'm driving it with no fear. God is amazing. I was so confident with driving that I continued driving all the way to the outskirts of Bossier City, Louisiana. It was about 10:00-11:00 pm when I found a hotel to get some sleep and something to eat. The next morning, I was up early.

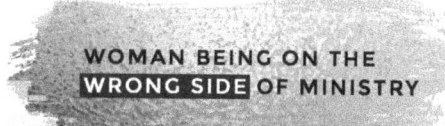

WOMAN BEING ON THE WRONG SIDE OF MINISTRY

Anitra and I showered, ate breakfast, and fueled up the truck. I was feeling confident, so I took the first morning drive. It was about 8:00 am when we started out and it was not long before I found myself driving on a freeway bridge going into what looked like a figure eight.
I thought I was going to lose control of the truck. Cars were passing me and cutting in front of me as I was having a complete meltdown. I am afraid of bridges and fast-moving traffic and my anxiety was out of control. Anitra kept talking, helping me find an exit.

We finally found an exit, and I exited. There was a gas station to the right, so I turned in and I heard something pop. I pulled in and straightened the truck. Still having anxiety, I shut off the truck and we both got out to see what had popped. The car towing hitch had broken in two. I was done. I couldn't think, so Anitra asked if there was a one eight hundred number I could call. I never had to deal with anything like this before in my entire married life, so I was out of control and I did not know what to do. I thank God for Anitra. I called the truck rental and they said that someone would be there in about 90 minutes.

About two hours later, they showed up with another car carrier. I was so relieved to see that extra car carrier. The gentleman informed us that we would have to unstrap and remove the car ourselves. Yes, you already know that I had no idea how to do that. I was feeling so hopeless and stupid that I was starting to cry and scream and just have another meltdown.

Anitra was definitely the calm one. She asked the gentleman to show her what to do and she did it. I drove the car off, they hitched up the extra car carrier, reloaded the car, tied it down and we were on our way. It was about 10:30 am when we got back on the road, with Anitra driving of course. She was merging onto the freeway when I noticed smoke coming from the car tow. She pulled off the freeway. The traffic was moving so fast and there was no way we could get out to see what was wrong with the car carrier. Traffic was not letting up and every 18-wheeler that passed us just rocked the truck. We had to call 911, and they sent a policeman to slow the traffic down so we could get off of the freeway again. Wow, by then we knew the drill. The left tire rim cover was bent, causing the tire to smoke.

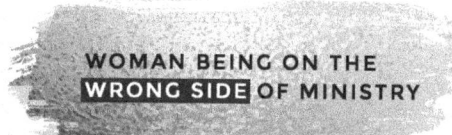

We pulled into a convenience store and called the truck rental company again. We knew it was going to be awhile, so we took it upon ourselves to take the car off the carrier to save time. It took about one and a half hours before the guy arrived with another carrier. I immediately checked out the carrier. I did not want any more delays. There was a gentleman at the store that assisted us with the car tow, who seemed to know that area really well.

Finally, we were ready to go, but there wasn't enough room in which to turn around the truck to get back on the freeway. The gentleman suggested that we circle the hotel and then exit, which seemed logical for two ladies with a big truck and a car in tow. We did just that, only to realize that the truck was too tall to pass under the hotel covering. Anitra and I both tried to back the truck out, but we could not do it. The hotel owner was upset with us, but we couldn't get the truck out. I was losing it again. We were experiencing so much warfare, I didn't know what else to do. We had lost so much time that day. Eventually, the hotel manager called a friend that was a truck driver to come see if he could help us.

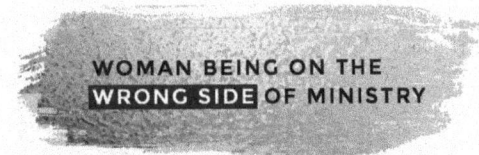

He backed the truck all the way out and turned it around, so that all we had to do was get on the freeway. I couldn't thank that man enough. I offered to pay him, but he said no. I offered to feed him and he said that he was ok, he just wanted to help. I praise God for sending us an angel to help us in our time of distress.

As Anitra was driving, she wasn't talking much. She honestly stayed far away from me. I was so glad to be getting on the road again and I wanted to express my relief, but my friend was not having it. She shut me down immediately and told me not to talk. I tried again to express myself and again she shut me down. Her instruction to me was to take my happy pill and go to sleep. I think that she was tired of me for that day, and after I had some time to think back, I didn't blame her at all...I needed to go to sleep. lol. That evening we made it to the outskirts of Alabama before bedding down for the evening to get some much-needed rest. After our ordeal in Des Moines, Louisiana, Anitra renamed it Voodoo City and she vowed never to stop in that city again. I agree!

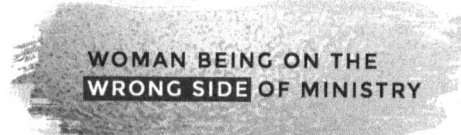

The next morning, we awoke refreshed and prayed up as we started driving through Alabama to the great state of Georgia. After fueling up, I asked a gentleman about any freeway bridges on the way to Alabama. He told me it was straight roads ahead, so I took the first drive because I needed to regain my confidence after the meltdown of the day before. I was determined to make the devil a liar. The enemy had launched an attack against me from the time my spirit was released. You see, the enemy never wanted me to leave. He wanted me to stay there and struggle, but I heard God tell me after my divorce to leave, and that is what I did. It was a battle as you can see, but I am one determined child of God. I might bend but I won't break, and every attack the enemy sends, I reverse it back to the sender. I had to start speaking in the atmosphere that no weapon formed against me shall prosper, and that the greater one was in me!

After driving through Alabama, we entered the great state of Georgia. I was so happy to see Georgia that I forgot to take a picture for Anitra.

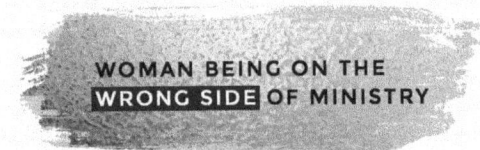

WOMAN BEING ON THE WRONG SIDE OF MINISTRY

Wow, she was pouting so bad about not getting a picture of the Georgia sign that we got off at the next exit to enter Alabama again to get back on 20 East to enter Georgia again so I could get her a picture...the smile on her face was priceless. The traffic in Atlanta was not as bad as my previous experiences. Anitra was handling it very well. She drove to the outskirts of Atlanta before fueling up again, and I drove us into Augusta. We arrived a little after midnight on the second of February, 2018 to what I now know was the beginning of my recovery. I will be the first to tell you that this test / trial was the hardest test I ever had to overcome, but, because of the years invested, I am a living testimony that Our God is a Healer and He Will Restore The Years That The Devil Stole From Me With Better, And He Will Give Me Back Double For My Trouble!

I am a grateful soul today! My God brought me from betrayal, abandonment, and divorce. My ministering angels: Mr. Jerry Smith (Papa) and Mother Bonita Smith (Meema), welcomed me into their home with open arms. They were my healing balm. They gave me a room to sleep in and food to eat.

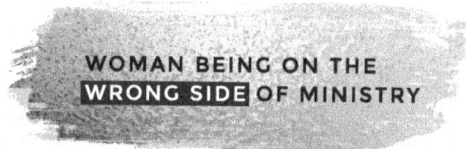

They constantly prayed, encouraged and loved me when I was weighed down and frustrated with my progress. Day by day, month by month, I was beginning to make progress toward recovery. I had to start by saying that I was divorced, single and free. I was giving voice to my confession and, because I agreed with the testimony of my heart. I was piecing my life back together. I was regaining my strength to walk into my singleness with the Lord as my source of living. I realized that it was only heavy because I had not moved on to the next chapter of my life. I have now taken back my joy, peace, identity, power, calling and My Anointing.

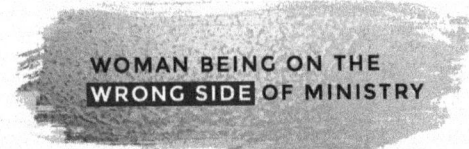

Chapter 12
The Conclusion
DOING THE WORD

Ecclesiastes 12:13

Let us hear the conclusion of the whole matter: Fear God and keep His commandments: for this is the whole duty of man.

In the months to come, after divorcing the man that said "I (verbally) abused him" ... I began to pick up the pieces of my life and journey to a place that I was not originally from, with God's amazing grace, the love of family and friends, pastors and their wives, spiritual mothers and fathers of the faith near and far who were my sources of prayers, strength and financial support as I continued my Journey to what I now call My Recovery. I cannot begin to thank them enough for their prayers and their genuine concern for my wellbeing and state of mind. I was experiencing a lot of demonic attacks, and I had to do a lot of fasting and spiritual warfare. I stayed in the face of God continually and trusted Him for a favorable outcome in every situation, plot, plan, and slanderous attack that was launched against me.

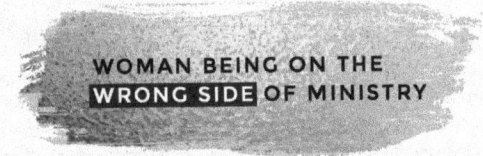

It took me months to recover from my divorce, and there were times when I thought that I was good only to relapse, but, as time and GOD heal all wounds, I am a living witness. I have come to accept some truths about myself and these truths have made me free. On June 20, 2018, I wrote this to my ex-husband Jack:

Forgiveness

Wed., June 20, 2018, 10:40 AM

Mr. Jack,

I am taking this time to extend My Forgiveness to You... Not because of the numerous affairs that you committed with other women while we were still married, I instantly Forgive you for those... that Forgiveness for Your Adultery was easy.

Life happens and it could had been me needing you to Forgive me for such an act... but Thank God for keeping me Faithful to My vows. I'm extending this Forgiveness to you because you abandoned and neglected me for over six months while we were still married.

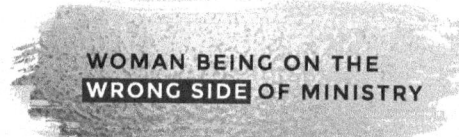

No Money for Food, Medicine, or House Bills, that was the worst... not to mention All your slander of My Name over the entire City. I Forgive You For Them All... You no longer hold the power over me that has hindered me from completing My book, and I am free from your control and I am released to move Forward in My God given Assignment to build up the Kingdom of God one soul at a time. I thank you for this awesome test that has led me to discover this Amazing powerful woman that is embarking on her New journey to a New Beginning. I hope you are happy now... because I have Joy and I am Free.

Linda Yvette Mickens Foster

As his Wife, I must confess that I was a very stressed out wife. I was never enough, or could never measure up to his expectations. I must confess that we shared two different values. I'm more financial. I was the one who rendered to God and our household needs first. Jack was very materialistic, and he would rob Peter to pay Paul.

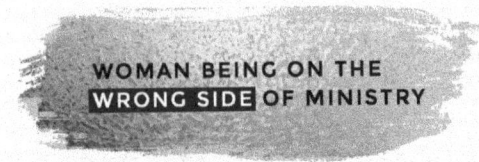

He always had to be the center of attention, the best dressed, have the latest gadgets, the nicest car, and the biggest house, and of course everyone had to like him and speak well of him. He could never see his actions. He is very charming, and the only thing that was abused was his ego.

As a Mother, of three sons, who I raised to be their brother's keeper, to look out for each other, and to love each other regardless of the situation, I must confess that I was very over protective and I had zero tolerance of any disrespect or not getting along with each other. If you ask any of my sons, they would all agree. As their mother, I acknowledge that I may not have made all the right decisions for them, but I believe that I trained / raised them up in the way that they should go, and that I made the best decisions for each of them in their individual passion. I only wanted the best for each of them, and I must say that I am proud of my sons and their accomplishments, and I know there is more to come as they continue to strive in the fear of the Lord.

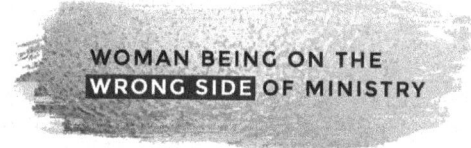

As a First Lady, this was one of the hardest assignments as a Christian woman that I have endured. Being a pastor's wife, I have a great passion for pastor's wives. I have served in this position for over twenty-four years. It takes another pastor's wife in most cases to relate. I was always the one that had to do the extra, to avoid getting the extra. I could read books, talk to other first ladies, pray and fast, and to some, I would never measure up to their potential. I was always seeking out ways to improve my character, my dress, my speech and my overall personality. Several women would tell me that I did not act like a pastor's wife. Well, this position didn't come with a standard operating manual, so I tried to measure up to their standards. Some would say, you need to wear hats, so I would buy hats, and then it was something else. Even Jack told me that some women at the local post office in my hometown told him that if he divorced me, he would pack his church out. How ignorant is that, but ask me if he defended our marriage vows and I will tell you NO! I know now that Jack fed on my insecurities and failures, and the more he could make me the problem, that is exactly what he did.

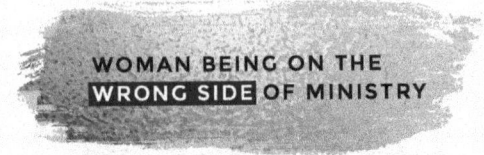

WOMAN BEING ON THE WRONG SIDE OF MINISTRY

The hardest thing about being a first lady was always feeling like I was not appreciated by Jack, and his spirit of competition to outshine everyone and everybody, including me, would eventually destroy us from the inside.

As a Pastor/ Co-Pastor/ Executive Pastor

I wore a lot of hats at our church. We founded our ministry in October of 1997. I helped him from the beginning until he barred me from attending services there in September of 2017. I was the church administrator, church manager, program planner, etc. Jack appointed me to do all of these assignments; he would give me an assignment and I would not rest or sleep until they were completed. I made preaching easy for him, he knew that I loved him and that I would do whatever it took to assure him that I was all in. There was nothing that he wanted that he did not get. I would make it happen. For 24 years in ministry, I was jumping from work, church, family, counseling, programs and church plays, just like the songwriter said, he wanted to put more on you than you could bear. Another songwriter wrote a song that said:

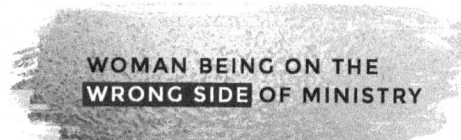

I never would have made it without you...I can stop right here and give God all the praise. I am alive today because of God's Grace!!! So, let us hear the conclusion of this matter: In a marriage there are always three sides: my side, his side, and God's Commandments. I am not perfect, and I definitely had my share of faults in this marriage. I know for a fact that I was not the easiest person to live with, but neither is anyone else.

Proverbs 21:9 It is better to dwell in a corner of the housetop than with a brawling woman in a large house.

I know some men who will take this scripture out of context to justify or cover up their sinful nature, but a wise pastor's wife made a statement one time in reference to this scripture, that she was just curious as to why the woman was brawling. I thought about this scripture even more when I started going through my divorce. I was always within earshot of all the slanderous accusations that Jack said about me, and at times I did try to explain my side or make sense of it. Then, I remembered that wise mother's question: Why was she brawling?

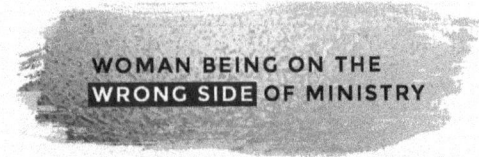

In defense of 80% of wives, I will quote a saying I heard that simply says "Happy Wife...Happy Life!" I've been around and have counseled many couples with and without Jack. I can say for a fact that, if there is any brawling coming from that home, as my grandfather would say, "something in the milk isn't clean." I know that with some wives, there is some brawling, but not from the wives that are mentored by the women of old who know how to keep a home and a man. I still want to know, just like mother, why she was brawling. I am guilty of being a brawling woman in my marriage and now I know why. I thank God for delivering me from a stressful marriage that I would have had to continue to be in to this day, had I not seen what I saw with my own eyes, but before that, I believed that all things are possible to those who believe. For 34 years, I believed. I did not say that we did not have our share of problems: money, church, relationship, communication, intimacy, you name it, we had it.... In the Word, God gave commandments to the husband and wife, and I'm going to list several from the husband and wife, so let's examine the conclusion of this matter:

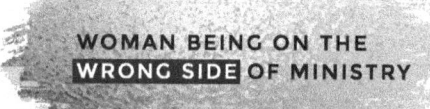

WOMAN BEING ON THE WRONG SIDE OF MINISTRY

The characteristics of a God-Fearing Husband is that he will:

1. Be a commandment keeper.
2. Desire to obey God and obey His Word.

Husbands have the responsibility to love and honor their wives.

1. Ephesians 5:25 - Love your wife as Christ loved the church.

I believe that at one point, Jack loved me, but not like Christ loved the Church. I loved him enough to fight for our marriage.

2. Ephesians 5:28 - So ought men to love their wives as their own bodies. He that loveth his wife loveth himself.

I know now that it was impossible for Jack to love me because, at some point in our marriage, he stopped loving himself.

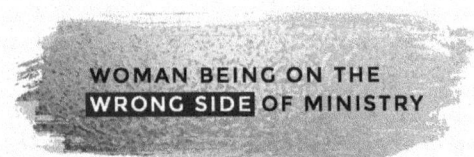

3. Colossians 3:19 Husbands, love your wives, and be not bitter against them.

At times, I think we were not nice to each other. Jack had a spirit of sarcasm and arrogance that was very annoying to me. At home, I would share with him how he would belittle me in front of others, he was always sorry, but with no change in behavior.

4. Proverbs 5:20 And why wilt thou, my son, be ravished with a strange woman, and embrace the bosom of a stranger?

I believe all men, including Jack, at some point have been enticed by women, just look at how my marriage ended and the time it took for him to remarry.

5. Hebrews 13:4 Marriage is honourable in all, and the bed undefiled: but whoremongers and adulterers God will judge.

Jack's adultery caused our divorce while he was still pastoring the church.

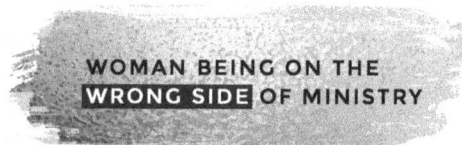

The wife will fulfill hers as well:

1. Ephesians 5:22-24 Wives submit yourselves unto your own husbands, as unto the Lord. **23** For the husband is the head of the wife, even as Christ is the head of the church: and he is the saviour of the body. **24** Therefore as the church is subject unto Christ, so let the wives be to their own husbands in everything.

I submitted to one man for thirty-four years of my young life. I dedicated myself to serve him and respected him as my husband, provider and protector. At times, I stressed about finances, the church and the members. I would take my frustration out on Jack, knowing that he was not the problem, but I was hoping he would open up and share anything with me just to have some spiritual interaction with him.

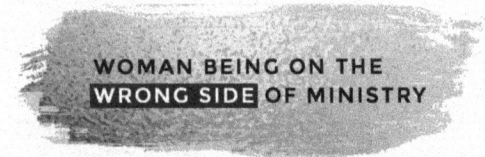

2. Ephesians 5:33 Nevertheless let every one of you in particular so love his wife even as himself; and the wife see that she reverences her husband.

It took me a minute to ponder this one. I knew that I loved my husband, but I know I didn't always reverence him with a deep respect. As I reflect on my lack of reverence to him, I definitely needed more grace. I instead spent most of my time doing ministry and not doing ministry to him. I believe this was an open door to his infidelity.

3. 1 Peter 3:5-6 For after this manner in the old time the holy women also, who trusted in God, adorned themselves, being in subjection unto their own husbands: **6** Even as Sara obeyed Abraham, calling him lord: whose daughters ye are, as long as ye do well, and are not afraid with any amazement.

I received a lot of wise advice from the women of old. I was a very caring wife, thinking I was fulfilling my wifely duties, only to discover that his needs were more than what I could provide.

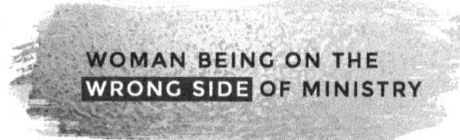

4. Colossians 3:18-19 Wives submit yourselves unto your own husbands, as it is fit in the Lord. **19** Husbands, love your wives, and be not bitter against them.

Submission was not hard to do but challenging at times. I thought I was being submissive to Jack, but I guess it was harder for me to submit to him with all the thoughts that were preoccupying my mind.

So, in closing, I found myself on the Wrong Side of Ministry, because I accept now what I knew then in 1997, that I was chosen by God to serve His people, but instead, I served my ex-husband's desires more. I personally cared for the things of the world as they related to Jack, catering to his worldly desires was a ministry that needed a lot of attention. I allowed "MY" Martha spirit to cloud my judgement. I really wanted to protect my marriage, and the very thing I tried to protect, I lost... because I served the creature more than the creator, who is blessed forever. Jack, on the other hand, immediately remarried about two months after our divorce. I'm happy that he has found true love and I wish them both longevity in their marriage.

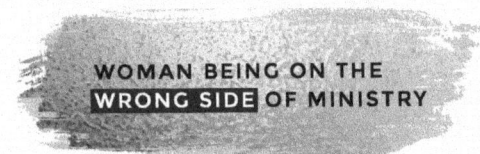

4. Colossians 3:18-19 Wives submit yourselves unto your own husbands, as it is fit in the Lord. **19** Husbands, love your wives, and be not bitter against them.

Submission was not hard to do but challenging at times. I thought I was being submissive to Jack, but I guess it was harder for me to submit to him with all the thoughts that were preoccupying my mind.

So, in closing, I found myself on the Wrong Side of Ministry, because I accept now what I knew then in 1997, that I was chosen by God to serve His people, but instead, I served my ex-husband's desires more. I personally cared for the things of the world as they related to Jack, catering to his worldly desires was a ministry that needed a lot of attention. I allowed "MY" Martha spirit to cloud my judgement. I really wanted to protect my marriage, and the very thing I tried to protect, I lost... because I served the creature more than the creator, who is blessed forever. Jack, on the other hand, immediately remarried about two months after our divorce. I'm happy that he has found true love and I wish them both longevity in their marriage.

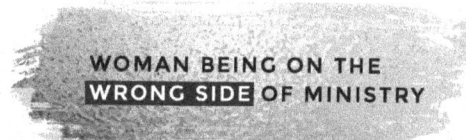

WOMAN BEING ON THE WRONG SIDE OF MINISTRY

As for me, I'm content with my singleness for now. After the completion of writing this book, I renewed MY Trust, Faith, and Commitment to the Calling of God on my life to serve the people of God. I have reconnected to My assignment to Pastor. I have found a New Freedom to Minister through my life-changing experiences as I am evolving in My Passion to Mentor and Coach Women and Men from all walks of life, to assist them in discovering their Real Worth, Real Potential, Real Purpose and Real Destiny. I pray that after reading this book of my journey thus far, that you will feel a sense of urgency to right every wrong practice in your marriage and your church. Seek God through praying and fasting so that you may be delivered from yourself, and be sure to Forgive Yourself, and everyone that was affected so that God can use you to share your testimony to all who will hear.

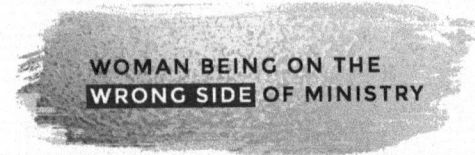

About this Book

Being on the wrong side of ministry: This book will take you on the journey of my life from a child growing up, chronicling notable events that shaped my life to being a wife of thirty-four plus years, a pastor's wife of twenty-four plus years serving side by side in ministry. I am grateful to God that he trusted me to go through this devastating test of betrayal and abandonment. I pray that this book will first of all inspire the reader to never put anyone or anything before God, second that they will be quick to forgive, get professional counseling from a Spirit led therapist, and start their process of healing to become a healthy person again. This book will give the reader insight into my life, and awareness of the patterns of lies and deception that I experienced from my ex-husband's betrayal.

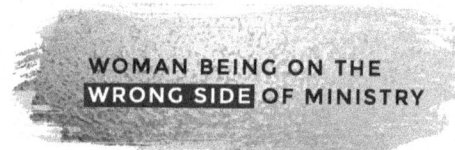

About the Author

Linda Yvette Foster is a devoted Christian woman, mother and grandmother who is full of virtue, wisdom, love and passion for everyone that she meets. She is known for her no-nonsense way of approaching issues that concern women who are discouraged and hurting; she empowers them to reach their full potential in God. She has served as Pastor/Executive Pastor, First Lady, Mother and Overseer of the Women's Ministry. She has an anointing in deliverance that will set the captives free. She encourages men and women to pursue their God-given passion. She is an anointed and gifted exhorter/worshipper who loves to usher the people of God into the presence of the Lord. She is an Entrepreneur, self-employed Cosmetologist and the owner/manager of Styles By Linda Exclusive Hair Care Salon.

Pastor, Visionary, Leadership, Empowerment, Passion: Speaker and Coach

For booking information email: thelisteningcoach20@gmail.com

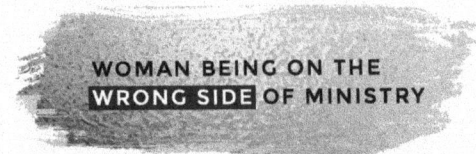

Book Endorsements

Blue Eyes, My Babysitter, but most of all, my inspiration to serve, fight and be the voice for those who cannot and often times are not allowed to speak for themselves or for others. As we were taught by the words of Papa Odell "An Empty Wagon Makes A Lot of Noise." Which is not the wagon that you possess, you have always been a light, beacon and a moderator of peace! WE know the story and support your calling to share. Remember Christ is not an impotent, weak, unresponsive, or incompetent force. He is a GOD of Power. He is a life-changer. He is able to affect circumstances and situations. Know that he has never been behind or on your side, he has always been in front leading you on this tour of what we accept as life.

South Carolina House of Representative

House District 122 Hampton, Jasper and Beaufort

Rep. Shedron Williams

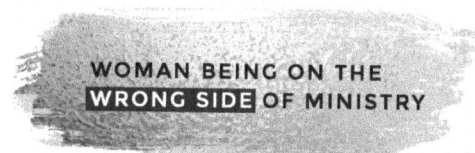

This book written by **Linda Y. Foster** can help and encourage others how to endure, persevere and overcome challenges in their lives. It's not just a retelling of her story but this book shows the reader how God can take you through the darkness and shine the light as you trust Him to help and guide you to safety.

Linda Y. Foster takes the reader on a compelling journey that brings transparent insight into the world of a Pastor's wife as she battles the pain, sorrow, and grief that she goes through with the help of God.

Toni Scott, MS, MHC,

Founder/President of

"A Woman of Destiny" Ministries

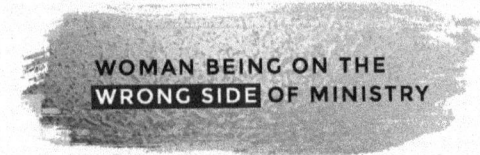

I first met **Linda Y. Foster** and her family while stationed in Giessen, West Germany approximately thirty-three years ago. I witnessed her rise from newborn believer to Co-Pastor and Executive Pastor of a thriving church. She has always demonstrated the epitome of leadership and hospitality. One of the things that I have always appreciated about her was her ability to be honest, and to stand up for right. I have always known Linda to stand firm in her teaching and ministering of the doctrine of the Lord Jesus Christ. As a Licensed Marriage and Family Therapist, I believe "Being on the Wrong Side of Ministry" is a must read for both men and women pursuing a path towards professional Christian ministry. In her book, Linda describes many pitfalls that hinder those called to serve, and if heeded, her book can assist the reader in avoiding mistakes that are routinely experienced in ministerial practice. In her writing, she has taken the reader along with her on her path of challenges and recovery. She has provided thoughtful insight into her own and common mistakes made in the Body of Christ as we endeavor to pursue the will of the Lord.

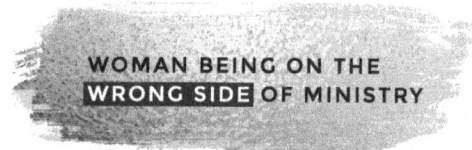

My sister has demonstrated humility and honesty by looking inward towards herself, as she crafted a book, that if read, will help many in the church achieve the Lord's Will for their marriages and professional lives.

Rev. Dr. Leo Daniel Jeffero, Jr.,
Th.D., MC, LMFT

Linda Y. Foster speaks with a vibrant compassion that will keep you from or rescue you out of family and relational pains and heartbreaks. This book is not an option... it is a must have, because you or someone you know and love needs this right now! This book will encourage you, motivate you, and instruct you.

Linda is known for her "truth, transparency, and timing!" This writing is from the heart of a survivor while walking and living the process! While speaking truth to power, she exposes her hurt and pain, and yet gives us hope in knowing that there is hope in the Word of God!

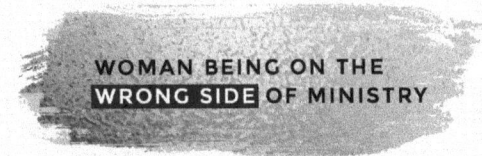

To the hurting, broken, abandoned, and neglected women, I encourage you to embrace this God-sent writing of hope and healing. But let me caution you to get ready for some uncomfortable, yet necessary truths, that will challenge your traditional comfortable church ideas and experiences. Linda Y. Foster's writing is Real, Raw, and Rewarding to the reader.

This is a very thought-provoking and life-changing book to those who read it with an open heart and mind, and I highly recommend it!!!

Bishop Timothy R. Cole

Senior Pastor / Founder

Rehoboth International

(The Love Center)

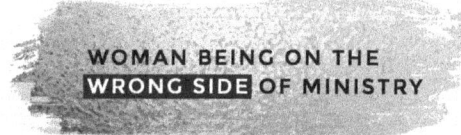

WOMAN is a book that will empower the souls of many women who can relate to the writers in this story of losing their power of not being good enough. Linda Yvette Foster takes you on a journey of her life from her happy childhood to her accomplished adolescence to being led down a dark twisted road of deception and betrayal. She speaks about her 34 years of marriage and 24 years of Ministry being married to an imposter being on the wrong side of ministry only to be abandoned and left alone fighting for her Life. Until she found her courage and love for God to reclaim her Power Back.

Yvonne D. Hoskey

Chef Hoskey

Around the world under one roof

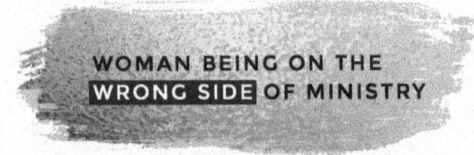